The Colosseum Book

To my walking companions and equipment
at the Colosseum, and to our guide

The Colos seum Book

Nunzio Giustozzi

Electa

Contents

The Colosseum. An Icon   11

I   A Miniature Amphitheatre   14
II   Blood and the Arena, the Fame of the Gladiator   42
III   The Christian Colosseum   76
IV   By Moonlight, Posing for the Grand Tour   116
V   The Symbol of an Empire   164
VI   A Myth of Our Time   192
VII   Cine-Colosseum   238

Bibliography   251

"The Colosseum is not only a monument, a machination of brick and boulder: it is a beast. It reproduces; its formidable stone has a fierce, reddish-brown and carnal quality; it is wild, seemingly a thing out of the forest, still in the wide open space, dazzled and silently furious."

At the end of the day there is not much separating the literary vision of Giorgio Manganelli and the image that a master of action painting like William G. Congdon visually gives us of the same monument: the Colosseum is there in its great presence, and yet mysterious. An icon so present in Western consciousness and imagination that facing it again, without retracing roads so well trodden that they are predictable, is a daunting undertaking.

Yet how to escape from such an arduous task in front of the success of one form of such strength so as to itself constitute the image of the city, as if the circularity of its form alone was enough to bring all the sensations and emotions, which for most visitors to Rome are destined to settle in the memory of an unforgettable experience, within a vortex of memory.

If it were not so we could not explain why, with symmetrical proportions, the increase in the number of tourists coming to Rome in recent years accurately follows the percentages of the Colosseum, or why over half of all those coming deem a visit to the Flavian Amphitheatre essential.

Hence the desire then, to investigate not only the history or symbolic strength of a place, which also brings forth bullies from the pages of the book, but also to collect the testimonies of how much this monument has caught the imagination of artists, painters, sculptors, architects and also writers, who have each wished to interpret the extraordinary nature of the Colosseum in their own way.

This volume has the audacity and honour to vividly illustrate some itineraries, of the many which are viable, on the post-ancient fortune of the amphitheatre: the building as an architectural model, the gladiator legend, its Christianisation, its re-use as ideological propaganda by totalitarian regimes and the perception of the monument in the 20th and 21st centuries. The wide and original array of images and literary pages, ordered in eloquent groups, and the presentation of numerous little known and unpublished materials, read in a continuous and coherent relationship with the monument, confirm the Colosseum as an exceptional source of inspiration for writers and artists until this day.

The in-depth analysis of the image of the amphitheatre over the centuries – with the overlying symbolic sense that ever accompanies it – and of its mythic component as well as its iconic exploitation, is today a cause for reflection in order to conceive and implement any strategic redevelopment project, and cultural proposals for using the Colosseum, in a mutual relationship with the image of the city which surrounds it.

The recent restoration of the exterior surfaces, together with the reopening of new routes on the inside, and the next project which will focus on the space of the arena, already allow the visitor the most up to date and complete vision of the monument. But it remains to take a major step towards improving the relationship between the Colosseum and Rome, after the final liberation from traffic which for a century imprisoned it and isolated it from its surroundings. It comes to thinking back to the *Piazza del Colosseo* – never conceived as a *piazza* but rather as a node of roads – which is today paradoxically one of the *piazze* most visited by citizens and tourists, as a space in which to finally live, without the nightmare of queues and commercial aggression. A plan which will rediscover the true dimension of the monument in relation with the city, A great new space for Rome, and her inhabitants.

Francesco Prosperetti
Superintendent

The Colosseum. An Icon

"Everybody knows the picture of the Coliseum; everybody recognises at once that "looped and windowed" band-box with a side bitten out".

Mark Twain, *The Innocents Abroad*, 1869

The vivid aphorism of the American writer already contains the modernity of approach to a monument that has always played at being a star, having the certain *physique du rôle*. All the prerequisites have over the centuries been reinforced by crowds of scholars who have designed an archaeological physiognomy truer to the real Colosseum thanks to documentary research, reliefs and excavations which have continued to this day. It is no wonder, therefore, that this book does not speak of the Flavian Amphitheatre, of how games were held in the Imperial Age and of their political and social significance, of the Medieval transformations and its reuse, of the Colosseum of the Popes, of the important nineteenth century restorers, of its life in the urban context if not in the "cultural" reflection that the long history of the building has projected into the screen of myth.

Yet of the most famous and among the most visited monument in the world we do not even know the name of the architect we see squaring off the heavens and the earth, a nude ideal on the frontispiece of an essay of *antiquaria* published a little before 1500. Alma-Tadema imagined a mature man while sketching a diagram thoughtfully on the sand, committed to solving the thorny design issues given the scale of the enterprise, the nature of the terrain which was previously a lake and the rapidity with which it would be necessary to complete construction. The architect was already allegorically present, showing the roll with his design to Vespasian on the Baroque vaults of the Hall of Apollo at Versailles, of magnificence in magnificence.

The most impressive and best preserved monument of antiquity had already become an object of veneration in the fifteenth century by architects and painters (from Francesco di Giorgio Martini to Antonio and Giuliano da Sangallo, from Palladio to Juvarra and from Aspertini to Velázquez and Turner) in the research of the paradigms of the classical language, to be published in treatises and printed manuals such as that of Serlio, and to interpret details and proportional relationships in their projects: in Florence and Rome the canonic sequence in the use of the applied orders is for example reiterated in the Palazzi (Rucellai and Altemps to name the most famous), in the loggias of blessing and in the courtyards of the Lateran, San Marco and the nearby Palazzo Venezia (which was even built with travertine scavenged from the monument) like in the Paduan Casa Cornaro.

On a parallel road, thanks to its unique *silhouette* and hypnotic sequence of arches the Colosseum favoured the utopian fantasies of Filarete and many after him, and it is easily recognisable in the outstanding atmosphere of the silent *Ideal City* of Baltimore where the Colosseum makes its appearance in a new reality, paused with grace and calculation with the Arch of Constantine that stands beside it, remains classical and becomes modern. A tribute to this famous "perspective" can be found in the work of the British artist Victor Burgin, author of an installation created in 2014 on the invitation of the Lia Rumma Gallery of Naples/Milan which envisaged a six minute digital video and two large photographic prints in ink. In the empty city the rationalist geometries of the Casa del Fascio by Terragni in Como appear among today's ruins.

The trite and oft recited prophecy of the Venerable Bede had after all been averted by the papal restorations, as shown in a fresco from the Biblioteca Vaticana by a winged angel-genius who indicates the Stern buttress, within the bricks of which the collapse has been frozen in a still image of the collapse, which has been able to visually translate the concept of historical instance from Brandi's *Teoria*.

The *Alpini* had gone as far as the attic, climbing it as if a mountain, and appearing on the cover of a "Domenica del Corriere" from the '50s: then the exceptional nature of the demonstration would have elevated their undertaking like that of many others who instead have demonstrated in front of the Colosseum for every cause, exploiting the appeal of the place, which would soon become an unchallenged *brand* of publicity – who could forget that in which sun awnings suddenly spring from the line of archways, or the icon of a widespread CD burning program which recalls with a credible time portmanteau the earlier incendiary foibles of Nero – and of high and low communication?

That the Colosseum represents an inestimable and common patrimony of history and human culture is by now clear to everyone, Italians but especially foreigners who invade it every day and in any case leave traces of their presence: a visit to the monument – and the claims of Obama confirm this – still constitutes a sensational experience and it is not uncommon to hear people who regret and feel surprise at never having entered.

Cutting indeed was the 1912 satirical cartoon of the American humorist and illustrator Oliver Herford which immortalised the cultured and enlightened magnate J. Pierpoint Morgan: after plundering all the wonderful works of art in Europe, the banker arrived in Rome and decided to put his hands on the Colosseum, which was promptly nailed to the ground! On the other hand, did Totò not attempt to sell the Trevi Fountain? Another similar story, incredible but not excessively so, given the necessity to stabilise public debt, is told by Marcello Sorgi today: it has as its protagonist an Arab Sheik who held a passing fancy to disassemble the Colosseum and take it home. Ai Weiwei has also understood the amphitheatre in his installation, made of about forty maxi selfies with the middle finger raised – a universally irreverent gesture – towards the most iconic places in the world, as a protest against the established order, including the St. Peter's Basilica and the Great Wall of China, the only ones who can beat our Colosseum in popularity, which is a truly global theatre even today.

A Miniature Amphitheatre

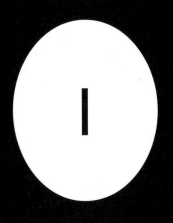

Many have been the images of the Colosseum from antiquity – just think of the bird's eye view of Rome which, in an intuitive perspective, would give volume to the topography of the city engraved on the marble slabs of the Severan Forma Urbis or in the models which surely existed – both in the public and private sector. An unusual relief from the Tomb of the Haterii, found in 1848 on the ancient Via Labicana, shows us simply the features of the Colosseum – which are made recognisable amongst the other famous buildings – the contract for which was awarded to a member of the family: truly a flagship project for the winning construction company. But the Romans could have the Colosseum in their hands, touching it and seeing it up close in all its parts, from an unusual point of view which even showed the fights in the arena among the crowds sat on the steps, on the splendid golden sestertii, silver denarii and bronze asses struck by the Senatorial and Imperial mints, several times, on special occasions. With its cylindrical shape and its charisma the image of the amphitheatre was well suited to being included on coins and medallions, and still today it is present on our copper plated 5 cent coin, perhaps a little devalued on a coin which is destined for doom. Since 1928 the outline of the Colosseum, although a little stylised and elusive, appeared on the Olympic medals until the Greeks in Athens, on occasion of the 2004 Games, managed to liberate themselves from the hegemony of Rome by replacing – in the spirit of Hellenic ideals of loyalty and fraternity – the amphitheatre dipped in blood with a Stadium. The bulk of the Colosseum dominated the urban fabric of the city, reproduced in a medal commissioned by Paul III Farnese to celebrate the embellishments for the Jubilee of 1550, a further visual document after the many 'portraits' of Rome, in which the Colosseum over the centuries had proudly emerged between the other symbols of the city: the Imperial 'bulls', luxury seals used by Frederick Barbarossa in the 12th century and, in 1328, Louis IV 'the Bavarian', and by two circles painted in small and large scale close together in time in the second decade of the fifteenth century. The first, a divine and surreal miniature, was made by the Dutch Limbourg brothers for the Duke of Berry; the second, an earthly fresco by the Sienese painter Taddeo di Bartolo, in the antechapel of the Palazzo Pubblico in Siena.

Small models of the Colosseum in wood or cork, delightful caskets and tobacco tins with micromosaics composed of extremely fine tesserae, in opus vermiculatum, with their nuances were among the most sought after souvenirs at a good market for travellers on the Grand Tour: in the romantic obsession for ruins, a pleasant substitute for the most popular paintings of vedutismo could come in the form of precious but bulky and fragile furniture, tables or porcelain service in which, as in the grandiose interiors of Pannini, they were associated, in a gallery of postcards, the most celebrated angles of Ancient and Modern Rome. Mutatis mutandis, in the joust of style, a situation not so far from the praise of kitsch in the junk of products destined for today's mass tourism, is a phenomenon aesthetically relevant for the photographer Martin Parr and many other authors. These products were the artisanal residue of a noble tradition Renaissance and Baroque modelling which was back in vogue in Rome and Naples in the second half of the eighteenth century, together with the archaeological research which fuelled the scientifically based construction, of three dimensional reproductions, and suggestive envois in watercolours, which were a fundamental means of spreading knowledge of Roman architecture in Neoclassical Europe and of iconographic sources for nineteenth century painters. Many scale replicas, not all of which survive, were dedicated to the most important and one of the best preserved monuments: the replicas of Antonio Chichi were particularly noted, an artist who probably worked in the workshop of Piranesi; also the fine example of Kassel, unique because a part of the monument is reproduced in the state in which it still was, with the buried exterior and floor of the arena before the nineteenth century works.

Every maquette of that time preserves an extraordinary documentary value, because it can volumetrically restore parts of the building which were later destroyed or modified.

The reconstruction of the amphitheatre of the Caesars begun by the carpenter Carlo Lucangeli in 1790, and completed by his brother in law Paolo Dalton in 1812, was undoubtedly an absolute masterpiece of its kind, precious for its perfect reproduction of the external perspective and internal galleries, and for the changes introduced as a result of excavations, was preceded by a model, now in Paris, which showed the state of preservation of the Colosseum at the time, one of the absolute masterpieces of its kind considered. It was seen and appreciated by Canova, by the French architect Joseph-Louis Duc during his stay in Rome, and by Raffaele Stern and Giuseppe Valadier, who declared the excellence of the work in a printed publication, and would soon direct the grand structural restorations with the the construction of the spurs which still 'underpin' the building, documented in the mid 19th century in yet another handmade model of the May brothers, preserved in the castle of Aschaffenburg.

These works modified the boundaries of the building conferring that iconic profile which burst into collective perception so much that we tend to reproduce it today in art or with every means or material that there is (from buildings to stacked cans…), almost as it originally was.

Since then – with the pause in the revival generated by the 1937 "Mostra Augustea della Romanità" – it has become preferable to entrust ever more faithful reconstructions of the building to graphic depictions – among which the best are those of Luigi Canina – and today in 3D, which take into account new data which derive from the progress of studies and research, despite never denying the efficacy of physical perception of volumes and spaces in a special way for new architectural projects.

Models of the Colosseum are highly accomplished at popular theme parks intended for "edutainment", such as the pioneering Italia in miniatura which was built in 1970 by the genius of Ivo Rambaldi in Rimini Viserba. The Colosseum, the symbol par excellence of grandeur, is metacartographical matched with other Italian glories with strange effects, which become Lilliputian in comparison with the visitor who passes through and above them, as Raffaella Carrà revealed in a celebrated, geographical television theme from 1978: the novelty of amusement parks for our country is so great that it even inspired a Donald Duck story. A glossy image of Alfred Seiland today re-establishes its value: in the systematic journey around the iconic "Colosseum", essentially a large creative design titled Imperium Romanum, the Austrian photographer is able to stop in the light and also elevate distorted 're-uses', which are also reduced and misinterpreted from that perspective, that form, for that fame, portraying the new, false Colosseums with clarity and metaphysical suspense in artificial paradises, in 'non places' where an amphitheatre can become a luxury hotel. Albeit with differing artistic results, Olivo Barbieri also follows this road of investigation of synthetic urban landscapes in Las Vegas as in Harbin, A Manchurian Chinese city, before a psychedelically magic Colosseum of ice.

Through a boorish search on the internet one discovers that the world is full of mimic Colossea: from incredible loggias of the Hotel Rome in Wisconsin which open onto nothing, to the redundant structures of the Hotel Coliseum in Georgia, while an unlikely lowered amphitheatre built from scratch to the state of ruin runs around the square of Fisherman's Wharf in Macau. The materials are improbable and the proportions wrong – it is a quotationism which inherits the worst of postmodern culture, and an ostentatious and luxurious accessory to build these monstra buildings, whereas for centuries the prototype had been reiterated with some finesse and coherence in the many plaza de toros and even in Wrigley Field, Home of the Chicago Cubs.

A detail of the marble relief from the
Tomb of the *Haterii* with the Colosseum,
1st century AD, Vatican City, Vatican
Museums, Museo Gregoriano Profano

In the sequence of Roman monuments ordered
by correct topographical sequence – perhaps those
in whose construction the developer, for whom the
tomb was destined, had participated – the building
with three rows of arches with an arched portico,
reserved for the entrance of the authorities,
surmounted by a quadriga without a chariot, perhaps
for lack of space, and statues in the arches has been
identified as the Flavian Amphitheatre. The lack of
the third floor, raised by Domitian, could indicate
an intermediary phase of construction, or it could
be a figurative simplification, common in this type
of representation.

Reverse of a bronze sestertius, with the oldest known image of the Colosseum, issued by the Emperor Titus to commemorate the inauguration, Rome mint, 80 AD.

The detail of the coin makes it possible to accurately identify the monuments of the valley after the Flavian arrangements, with the celebrated *Meta Sudans*, a luxury fountain by the amphitheatre, faithfully bringing back the original appearance of the building overflowing with spectators between the wedges of the cavea, rendered in schematic form for perspective needs. Thus we see the row of statues which adorned the upper galleries, which are today mostly lost, and the attic which incorporated enormous bronze shields which alternated with windows between the pilasters, and, at the top, the functional wooden beans which allowed the movement of the canopy.

Coin with the image of the Colosseum during a gladiatorial spectacle, issued in 222 AD during the reign of Severus Alexander, to celebrate the *dedicatio* of the amphitheatre to the gods, to which the three standing figures nearby allude, on occasion of the reopening of the monument after the damages sustained by a devastating fire which was caused by lightning strike.

In a 238 AD coin of Gordian III an aerial view reveals, in the vicinity of the Emperor, a duel in the arena between a bull and an elephant, on whose back we see a figure. The attention reserved to the monuments in the square – behind by the *Meta Sudans* we see the Colossus for the first time – could justify a new reason to celebrate, after the restoration of the building, the rearranging of the surrounding area.

Seal of the Emperor Frederick I Barbarossa, 1154-1155, gold, diameter 5.9 cm, Berlin, Staatliche Museen zu Berlin, Münzkabinett

A Miniature Amphitheatre

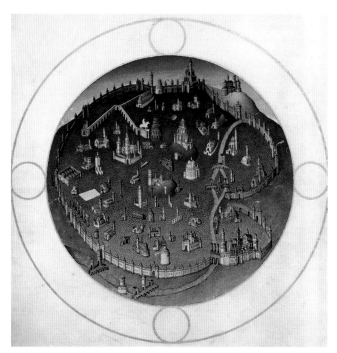

Paul, Jean and Hermann de Limbourg,
Rome in the *Très Riches Heures du Duc
de Berry*, fol. 141, 1411-1412, miniature,
Chantilly, Musée Condé

Taddeo di Bartolo, *Plan of Rome*,
1413-1414, fresco, Siena, Palazzo
Pubblico, antechapel

Carlo Lucangeli and Paolo Dalbono,
Model of the Flavian Amphitheatre, section
open from archway XLVI at the south
entrance, 1790-1812, wood and other
materials; total dimensions: height
82.5 cm, major axis 318 cm and minor
axis 261 cm; Rome, Special
Superintendency for the Colosseum
and the archaeological centre of Rome

The model consists of sixty distinct and autonomous
sectors, assembled in five concentric bands of
differing woods: the load-bearing sections are poplar;
the columns, the architraves and cornices are beech;
the capitals in extruding stucco; the transenne and
abaci upon the capitals are sheets of cut lead; the
archivolts are lead castings and the pulleys are bone
(Cinzia Conti).

The conservative and aesthetic intervention, begun in
2000 under the direction of Cinzia Conti, has
brought to light the original colour of the travertine
as it could have been appreciated at the end of the
eighteenth century, freeing the surfaces from the
white paint which had been considered a somewhat
plastic addition from the 1930's.

A Miniature Amphitheatre

Carlo Lucangeli and Paolo Dalbono,
Model of the Flavian Amphitheatre,
detail of the façade during restoration

Carlo Lucangeli and Paolo Dalbono,
Model of the Flavian Amphitheatre, detail
of the south entrance seen in open section

An engraving of the Count of Crozat,
published in 1729, which reproduces a
drawing of Giovanni da Udine, intended
to document the fine decoration of the
stucco finish in the central passage of the
northern entrance to the Colosseum

The restoration has highlighted the stucco
decoration, brought back on the basis of then
surviving fragments, and still visible until at
least the end of the sixteenth century, as is
attested by drawings and engravings.

A Miniature Amphitheatre

Carlo Lucangeli and Paolo Dalbono,
Model of the Flavian Amphitheatre,
perspective view of archway LXXVI
at the south entrance

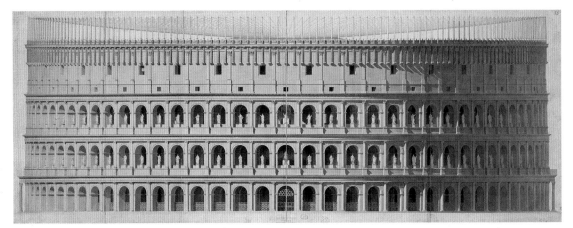

Louis-Joseph Duc, *Perspective of the Colosseum along the major axis*, 1831, Paris, École Nationale Supérieure des Beaux-Arts

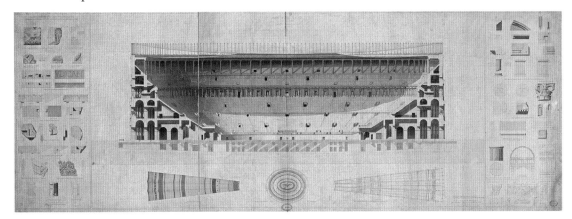

Louis-Joseph Duc, *Section of the Colosseum along the major axis*, 1831, Paris, École Nationale Supérieure des Beaux-Arts

A Miniature Amphitheatre

Louis-Joseph Duc, *The Corinthian Order of
the second floor of the Colosseum*, 1831, Paris,
École Nationale Supérieure des Beaux-Arts

Compared to the numerous nineteenth century paintings which invited a voyeuristic, sadistic and pseudo-erotic pleasure to enjoy the brightly coloured scenes in the arena, the "Victorian in a toga", as Alma-Tadema was sometimes called, this time transports us lovingly to a happy and light Rome, made of accurate environments which have helped fuel the archaeological imagination of entire generations of ancient scholars.

A Miniature Amphitheatre

Sir Lawrence Alma-Tadema,
The Colosseum, 1896, oil on panel,
112 x 73.6 cm, private collection

The restorer Pierino Di Carlo at work in the former Pantanella pasta factory, intent on shaping, under the wise guidance of the architect Italo Gismondi, the reconstructive model of the Constantinian city of Rome which was destined to be staged at the 1937 "Mostra Augustea della Romanità"; in the foreground we see the already complete model of the Colosseum. The work was alter expanded to incorporated the entire urban area within the Aurelian Walls, for the final layout which would be displayed in the Museo della Civiltà Romana in EUR in 1955.

Alfred Seiland, *Kolosseum–Modell. Italia in miniatura*, Rimini, Italy 2008

Olivo Barbieri, *Site specific_LAS VEGAS 05*

A Miniature Amphitheatre

Alfred Seiland, *The Colosseum, Caesars Palace, Las Vegas*, Nevada 2010

Alfred Seiland, *Hotel Colosseo.*
Europa-Park. Rust, Germany 2011

A Miniature Amphitheatre

Oliver Herford, Caricature of J. Pierpoint
Morgan, 1912

Roman workshop, Enamelled casket with view of the Colosseum, first half of the 19th century, micromosaic, Vatican City, Vatican Museums

Roman workshop, Snuffbox with nocturnal view of the Colosseum, after 1839, micromosaic, Vatican City, Vatican Museums

The *terminus post quem* for the dating of the refined object is obtained by the striking image of the restoration of the amphitheatre absent in the previous daytime view.

A Miniature Amphitheatre

Martin Parr, *Italy, Rome*, 2005

Olivo Barbieri, *Harbin*, China 2010

A Miniature Amphitheatre

Huang Yong Ping, *Colosseum*, 2007,
ceramic, topsoil and plants,
226 x 556 x 758 cm, Oslo, Astrup
Fearnley Museet

In the work of one of the pioneers of contemporary Chinese art, which abandoned the traditional formulaic approach to art by radically adopting the aesthetic and conceptual criteria of the West avant-garde, the position of the individual within an institutionalised context is symbolised by buildings representing power. His creations often revolve around metaphorical, cultural, religious and political oxymorons. In the sculpture Colosseum, the symbol of the Roman Empire becomes a large terracotta model, though controllable as a whole, where plants have grown on it. It has rather the same effect as the ruins, invaded by vegetation, in the views of the modern age, and implies an admission of the fragility of power and in the continuous dialogue between nature and civilisation.

Every work of Huang is an incentive to reflect on the human condition, and the strength of his art lies in the forms, the objects and in the materials that he assembles, and refers to the philosophical and anthropological traditions of both the East and West, articulating itself around its rejection of any cliched identity, political hegemony and ethnic differences.

Once upon a time a man set out to steal the Colosseum in Rome, he wanted to have it all for himself because he did not like having to share it with others. He took a bag, went to the Colosseum, waited for the guards to look another way and filled the bag with old stones before taking it home. [...]
But the Colosseum was always in its place, it lacked not even an arch: it would not have been more complete than this if a mosquito had worked to demolish it with its feet.

Gianni Rodari, *L'uomo che rubava il Colosseo*, from *Favole al telefono*, 1962

A Miniature Amphitheatre

Walt Disney, *Zio Paperone e la Giostra del Saracino*, extract from "Mickey Mouse", June 1992

The cover of *L'uomo che rubava il Colosseo* by Gianni Rodari, illustrated by Raffaella Bolaffio in the series "una fiaba in tasca" of Edizioni EL, 2011

The cover of *Il fantasma del Colosseo* di Geronimo Stilton edited by Piemme in 2016

Blood and the Arena, the Fame of the Gladiator

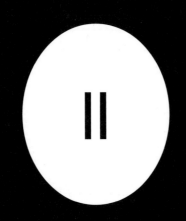

II

The stadium today, the arena yesterday for hours, between fifty thousand exultant Romans while in the background at the steps the gladiators performed in a grim game with death. Nothing has really changed. Fracas, shouts, the anger of yesterday and today. The amphitheatre, where the masses are with the Emperor, emerges as a place in which games that were not merely entertaining were held, but one which manifested the strength of a people who seems to crave only two things: *panem et circenses*. Perhaps then the people did not need these things, but today yes, to divert attention from real problems and to operate undisturbed.

The fame of the Colosseum – not the first building of its type but the model and the most majestic of all others built in the Roman World – has forever been tied to its function, to the crowds of men and those cruel spectacles. Though none of us has ever seen them with our own eyes, a boundless wealth of testimonies from the time (reliefs, sculptures, mosaics, paintings, lamps and ivories) and of objects – just think of the splendid parade weapons from Pompeii – re-evoke in their image those fights described in detail, with effective words from Latin, pagan and Christian authors, of Martial and Tertullian, even in ideological terms, to celebrate or more often, to condemn. The rousing rhetoric of those pages was bound to affect the reasoning, for example, of the English historian Edward Gibbon who, between the ruins of the monument on his Roman journey in the autumn of 1764, conceived his idea of the decline of the Empire, also in relation to the excess of Commodus. He did not hesitate to perform as a gladiator in hard fights which would meet the indignant condemnation of Alessandro Verri and the reflections of contemporaries: what took place in the amphitheatre is still presented as free reign given to cruel instincts, and manifestations of voyeurism and violence.

The seduction of the murky past of the Colosseum is rarely ignored by poets and writers of the nineteenth century, a century in which a large quantity and high quality historically inspired *pompier* paintings appeared, which give life with a certain verisimilitude and cinematic way to the lost *pathos*, the atmosphere of the place, the off-stage and the star quality of the gladiators – ruthless fighters yet consummate professionals – creating a cliché which soon became folklore that still exists today. Thus the American humorist and creator of *Tom Sawyer*, Mark Twain, revived the ancient *ludi* in a review of a gala evening which seems more suited to Broadway.

No other expression of Roman culture wields a popularity equal to that of gladiators in the Colosseum, a unique phenomenon of continuity, as a visual atlas which shows, aspiring to demonstrate, given that it keeps a precise place in our memory thanks to its massive presence in cartoons, cinema, video games and television series – such as the pulp-erotica *Spartacus: Blood and Sand*, broadcast to great acclaim in an Italy accustomed since the 1920's to the appreciation of the sensual charm of the partially nude gladiators of Giorgio de Chirico – in mass media and even the boisterous performances of the fighters, who are dressed and have studied the *retiarius* and the *murmillo*, are all the rage.

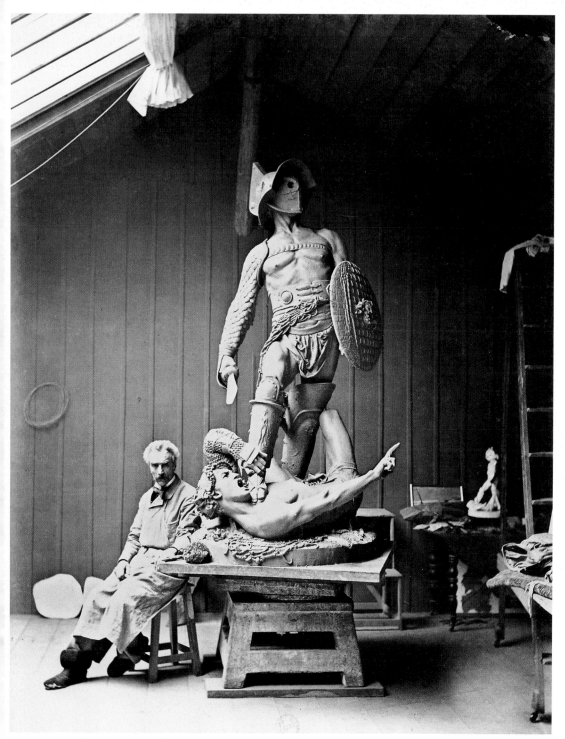

Anonymous, Gérôme in overalls sat
alongside *Gladiators*, c.1878, albumen
print, Paris, Bibliothèque nationale
de France, Département des Estampes
et de la Photographie

Workshop of Marco Zoppo, *Amphitheatre with Jousting Tournament*, before 1465, pen and ink on watercolour parchment, 341 x 240 mm, Modena, Biblioteca Estense

The legendary memory of ancient monuments, very much alive in the mid fifteenth century, probably inspired the fantasy of the draftsman who wished to set his jousting tournament, in which some courtiers assist, in an amphitheatre, and none other than the Colosseum, whose physiognomy is partly modified.

Marco Dente da Ravenna, *Fight between Dares and Entellus*, engraving by Giulio Romano, sixteenth century

The Colosseum, albeit in ruins, nevertheless remained the ideal setting for combat between burly heroes of myth.

Paris Bordon, *Gladiatorial combat*, c.1560,
oil on canvas, 218 x 329 cm, Vienna,
Kunsthistorisches Museum

Placed in an enclosure in the middle of the road,
the gladiators are framed by painted architecture,
including the Colosseum which indirectly taken
from the drawing of Serlio. For its scenic setting in
the canvas was conceived with a pictorial chronicle
of those events (stagings of triumphal arches, gaming
institutions, etc.) which took place on occasion
of the arrival of the rulers of European courts
(Michela Di Macco).

He plunged his hunter's spear also in a headlong-rushing bear, the king of beasts beneath the cope of Arctic skies; and he laid low a lion, magnificent, of bulk unknown before, one worthy of Hercules' might; and with a far-dealt wound stretched in death a rushing pard. He won the prize of honour; yet unbroken still was his strength.

Martial, *De Spectaculis*, 80 AD

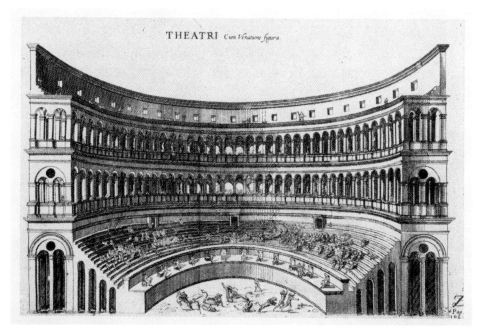

Onofrio Panvinio, *Theatri cum venatione figura*, from *De ludis Circensibus et de Triumphis*, 1681

Jacopo Lauro, *Ludi in Amphitheatro*, da *Antiquae Urbis Splendor*, 1699

Omnis Caesareo cedat labor Amphitheatro

Vincenzo Brenna, *Interior section of the Colosseum
with Spectators and a Mock Lion hunt*, 1769-1770,
pen and watercolour, 60 x 97.5 cm, London,
Victoria and Albert Museum

Vnum pro cunctis Fama loquatur Opus. Martial. de. Amphit-

Blood and the Arena, the Fame of the Gladiator

Stefan Bakałowicz, *The Gladiators before Entry*, 1891, oil on canvas, 66 x 98.5 cm, Saint Petersburg, State Russian Museum

A crowned beast; or perhaps, what we see is not exactly the crown, nor the beast hidden in the ground – are we not atop a ferocious place, the unfathomable lair of a nameless tyranny?

Tyrant; tyrants, men of blood and fury work towards the invention and discovery of this object-being. This stony beast was, perhaps, their dream, a happy nightmare, a proclamation of an imperial massacre; the Colosseum resembled those shady and powerful men; of them and their well organised violence, it preserves, proposes and reveals memory; the ancient violence that hailed from Rome will never die, as long as this wide open prison remains, wounded yet alive. [...]

By the palace, and the deceptively inviting doors, we think of the beasts that this beast welcomed in its prisons; darkly do those horrid games, in which imperial cruelty was allied to plebeian infamy, emerge before our eyes; an alliance that had to be in order to retain something of taste, even if there were Christians who suffered by renouncing Stefan Bakałowicz, *The Gladiators before Entry*, 1891, oil on canvas, 66 x 98.5 cm, Saint Petersburg, State Russian Museum

them; but I also think of the olives that were chewed two thousand years ago, whose stones were found along the route of the spectators. That small bone of the fruit has survived, has traversed the millennia, when not even the dust remains of those teeth, but the core is of the same matter as the amphitheatre. This lacerated tondo, this curve of incomparable hardness, this game of cavities and peaks and receptacle of a secret forest not so long ago, offers itself as the core, the unyielding heart of stupendous imperial brutality.

Giorgio Manganelli, supplement to the "Messaggero", August 1989

Sir Lawrence Alma-Tadema, *Caracalla and Geta*, 1907, oil on panel, 123.2 x 153.7 cm, private collection

This masterpiece, among the artist's most complex and painted with consummate mastery at the age of over 70, depicts the grandiose spectacle organised at the Colosseum in 203 AD by Septimius Severus for the awarding of the title of *Antoninus Caesar* to his son Caracalla, who we see behind the Emperor seated beside the consort Julia Domna. The Augusta, as is perhaps revealed by the damning letter of the handmaiden, aspired to have the same honour conferred upon her son Geta (later murdered by Caracalla). The latter, standing between the sisters, is appreciating the gladiatorial scene going on in the arena, echoed in the precious decoration of his toga. It is a particularly strategic move adopted in the *venationes* which the artist takes from the iconography of an ivory diptych. Alma-Tadema spared no effort in the calligraphic rendering, archaeologically reliable by the standards of the time, of the monument with fountains and altars, while on the steps one can recognise cushion hirers, vendors selling drinks and sweets for the more than two thousand five hundred spectators that have been counted in the painting.

Night had now completed the half of her silent course. The unclouded moon beamed from the zenith, and her light, floating over the immense pile of the Colisaeum, defined its form, broadly but faintly, and touched it into bolder relief where the illumined exterior was contrasted with the spacious vomitories, and the deep obscurity within the. arcades. The low night breeze waved the tangled wild plants and ivy over the crumbling walls; and the dark starry azure, seen through the ruinous arches, was like lustrous sapphire. The spectres, like a countless flock of wild doves, descending and resting on some rustic thatch, disseminated themselves over the vast edifice; and traversed the vaulted galleries and empty passages until they reached the topmost arch. I remained in the centre of the arena, contemplating the admirable spectacle…

On this spot, infamous by all the pangs and slaughter it has witnessed, human beings, for the sport of their fellow-men, were compelled to offer themselves to the talons of the lion. Here for your delight, ran the panting tiger, crushing in his rabid jaws the quivering limbs of his human victims: like you, pleased with this horrible repast. Not a grain of this sand but has drunk blood in those slaughters, fit only for savage contemners of the sufferings of humanity. Here, as the gladiator expired, you, skilful in distinguishing the various modes of the last agony, roared your applause, if he sunk and died in a graceful attitude, but hooted his convulsions with inhuman scoffs. And as if the common hazards of the gladiatorial combat palled upon the eyes of the barbarous vulgar, tasteful ornaments were invented to give the scene a festival and novel aspect: a diversity of swords and shields and fanciful manners of fighting, enhanced its variety. Sometimes the combatant advanced with a net and a dagger, and was to display his art by dextrously entrapping his adversary, and stabbing him while thus pinioned; or sometimes it was your pleasure to behold the victims engaging blindfolded, dealing or receiving wounds and death at a venture; at other times it pleased your caprice that puny dwarfs should engage in the fatal contests of the arena. How lofty and noble were the sentiments of your patricians, who, rising glutted from the banquet, decked themselves in gorgeous apparel, and reeling with Falernian…

Alessandro Verri, *Roman Nights*, 1782-1804

Jean-Léon Gérôme, *Pollice verso*, 1872,
oil on canvas, 96.5 x 149.2 cm, Phoenix,
Phoenix Art Museum

They are moments of tension inside the Colosseum rebuilt so accurately, thanks to several preparatory studies, that they even reveal the rays of light which passed through the canopies. To the presence of the Emperor, sat upon the Imperial balcony, the crowd who is in the grip of fanaticism demands that the winner kill the loser, is added the Vestals who appear on the right hand side of the painting: in the eyes of nineteenth century observers that cruelty is rendered even more repulsive by the fact that women are asking for this killing. The arena is littered with corpses, and death appears to be the inevitable fate of all gladiators. In the amphitheatre the decadence of the Romans seems to be symbolically condensed; to oppose this corruption there is a need of "pure" men, uncontaminated by the sins of the metropolis: in Henryk Sienkiewicz's novel *Quo Vadis?* (1896), this role is bestowed to the Ligians – the alter ego of the Poles, fellow countrymen of the writer [and the painter Siemiradzki who worked on the same

themes] – and to Maximus the Spaniard in the film *Gladiator* (Christian Mann).
The title of the painting linked to the image does not however resolve the dispute which academics have to settle, compared to the traditional interpretation, in which the Romans turned their thumbs to decree life or death in the arena.
The gladiators painted by the artist on his canvases at times become protagonists, isolated in the foreground, even from behind, making them stand out from the background, which is evident in the statues of gladiators, thanks to the attention given to accuracy in the rendering of their offensive and defensive equipment, obtained by studying the original weapons found in the Museo Archeologico Nazionale di Napoli and private collections, of which the author made life size copies to test on his models. He was then even able to clarify the use of the various elements of the equipment which until then remained obscure.

It is our duty to hate these assemblies and gatherings of the heathen, were it only that there the name of God is blasphemed; that there, every day, the shout is raised to set the lion upon us; that from there persecution begins; that there temptation has its base. What will you do when you are caught in that heaving tide of guilty voices? I do not suggest that you run any risk there of suffering from men – nobody recognises you for a Christian; but think well over it, what it means for you in heaven. Do you doubt but that at that very moment when the devil is raging in his assembly, all the angels look forth from heaven, and mark down man by man, how this one has spoken blasphemy and that has listened, the one has lent his tongue, the other his ears, to the devil against God? Will you not rather fly the chairs of the enemies of Christ, "the seat of the pestilences," the very overhanging air defiled with sinful cries? Granted that you have there something that is sweet, agreeable and innocent, some things that are excellent. No, one mixes poison with gall and hellebore; no, it is into delicacies well made, well flavoured, and, for the most part, sweet things, that he drops the venom. So does the devil; the deadly draught he brews, he flavours with the most agreeable, the most welcome gifts of God. So count all you find there – brave and honest, resounding, musical, exquisite, as so much honey dropping from a poisoned bit of pastry; and do not count your appetite for the pleasure worth the risk in the sweetness.

Tertullian, *De Spectaculis*, 200-212 AD

Jean-Léon Gérôme, *Ave Caesar, Morituri te salutant*, 1859, oil on canvas, 93.1 x 145.4 cm, New Haven (Connecticut), Yale, University Art Gallery

The work is probably inspired by a passage from the novel *The Last Days of Pompeii* by Edward Bulwer-Lytton, published in France in 1838, which describes in minute detail six fighters in the arena of which two gladiators come from Rome. Thanks to some advisors (architects and archaeologists), the portrayal of the Colosseum is fairly accurate, because it made use of the most recent acquisitions which hailed from the restorations of 1822. In this canvas the spectacular use of a panoramic scale is striking, since it places the observer on the ground almost as if he were an eyewitness lifting his eye towards the Imperial Box, and then up towards the canopies in a distortion of the ellipse through a forced perspective as far as the eye can see.

The title of the work, still in Latin, recalls a rare documented reference from the sources (Suetonius and Cassius Dio) to the phrase, soon to become a slogan of modern culture, which was perhaps ever uttered in the Colosseum as a greeting turned to face the Caesars. The painting also displays how much of the bodies of gladiators remained uncovered, exposed therefore to the blows of their adversaries with bloodshed assured, rather than in the custom of medieval joust, when knights competed fully protected in their coats of mail.

But every sentiment of virtue and humanity was extinct in the mind of Commodus. Whilst he thus abandoned the reins of empire to these unworthy favorites, he valued nothing in sovereign power, except the unbounded license of indulging his sensual appetites.

Commodus, from his earliest infancy, discovered an aversion to whatever was rational or liberal, and a fond attachment to the amusements of the populace; the sports of the circus and amphitheatre, the combats of gladiators, and the hunting of wild beasts.

The servile crowd, whose fortune depended on their master's vices, applauded these ignoble pursuits. The perfidious voice of flattery reminded him, that by exploits of the same nature, by the defeat of the Nemæan lion, and the slaughter of the wild boar of Erymanthus, the Grecian Hercules had acquired a place among the gods, and an immortal memory among men.

Elated with these praises, which gradually extinguished the innate sense of shame, Commodus resolved to exhibit before the eyes of the Roman people those exercises, which till then he had decently confined within the walls of his palace, and to the presence of a few favorites. On the appointed day, the various motives of flattery, fear, and curiosity, attracted to the amphitheatre an innumerable multitude of spectators; and some degree of applause was deservedly bestowed on the uncommon skill of the Imperial performer. Whether he aimed at the head or heart of the animal, the wound was alike certain and mortal.

The dens of the amphitheatre disgorged at once a hundred lions: a hundred darts from the unerring hand of Commodus laid them dead as they run raging round the *Arena*. Neither the huge bulk of the elephant, nor the scaly hide of the rhinoceros, could defend them from his stroke. Æthiopia and India yielded their most extraordinary productions; and several animals were slain in the amphitheatre, which had been seen only in the representations of art, or perhaps of fancy. In all these exhibitions, the securest precautions were used to protect the person of the Roman Hercules from the desperate spring of any savage, who might possibly disregard the dignity of the emperor and the sanctity of the god.

But the meanest of the populace were affected with shame and indignation when they beheld their sovereign enter the lists as a gladiator, and glory in a profession which the laws and manners of the Romans had branded with the justest note of infamy.

Edward Gibbon, *The History of the Decline and Fall of the Roman Empire*, 1776-1789

A lively and credible from Ridley Scott's *Gladiator* with Russell Crowe (USA, 2000) which refers to the paintings of Jean-Léon Gérôme. The following statement has been attributed to the director: "Those images spoke to me of the Roman Empire in all her glory and perversion. Ever since I knew I was hooked".

Seventeen or eighteen centuries ago this Coliseum was the theatre of Rome, and Rome was mistress of the world. Splendid pageants were exhibited here, in presence of the Emperor, the great ministers of State, the nobles, and vast audiences of citizens of smaller consequence. Gladiators fought with gladiators and at times with warrior prisoners from many a distant land. It was the theatre of Rome--of the world--and the man of fashion who could not let fall in a casual and unintentional manner something about "my private box at the Coliseum" could not move in the first circles. When the clothing-store merchant wished to consume the corner grocery man with envy, he bought secured seats in the front row and let the thing be known. When the irresistible dry goods clerk wished to blight and destroy, according to his native instinct, he got himself up regardless of expense and took some other fellow's young lady to the Coliseum, and then accented the affront by cramming her with ice cream between the acts, or by approaching the cage and stirring up the martyrs with his whalebone cane for her edification. The Roman swell was in his true element only when he stood up against a pillar and fingered his moustache unconscious of the ladies; when he viewed the bloody combats through an opera-glass two inches long; when he excited the envy of provincials by criticisms which showed that he had been to the Coliseum many and many a time and was long ago over the novelty of it; when he turned away with a yawn at last and said, "He a star! handles his sword like an apprentice brigand! he'll do for the country, may be, but he don't answer for the metropolis!". Glad was the contraband that had a seat in the pit at the Saturday matinee, and happy the Roman street-boy who ate his peanuts and guyed the gladiators from the dizzy gallery.

For me was reserved the high honor of discovering among the rubbish of the ruined Coliseum the only playbill of that establishment now extant.

Roman coliseum.
Unparalleled attraction!
New properties! New lions! New gladiators!
Engagement of the renowned
Marcus Marcellus Valerian!
For six nights only!
The management beg leave to offer to the public an entertainment surpassing in magnificence any thing that has heretofore been attempted on any stage. No expense has been spared to make the opening season one which shall be worthy the generous patronage which the management feel sure will crown their efforts. The management

beg leave to state that they have succeeded in securing the services of a

galaxy of talent!

such as has not been beheld in Rome before. The performance will commence this evening with a

Grand broadsword combat!

between two young and promising amateurs and a celebrated Parthian gladiator who has just arrived a prisoner from the Camp of Verus. This will be followed by a grand moral

Battle-ax engagement!

between the renowned Valerian (with one hand tied behind him,) and two gigantic savages from Britain.

After which the renowned Valerian (if he survive,) will fight with the broad-sword,

Left handed!

against six Sophomores and a Freshman from the Gladiatorial College!

A long series of brilliant engagements will follow, in which the finest talent of the Empire will take part. After which the celebrated Infant Prodigy known as

"The young Achilles,"

will engage four tiger whelps in combat, armed with no other weapon than his little spear!

The whole to conclude with a chaste and elegant

General Slaughter!

In which thirteen African Lions and twenty-two Barbarian Prisoners will war with each other until all are exterminated.

Box office now open.

Dress Circle One Dollar; Children and Servants half price.

An efficient police force will be on hand to preserve order and keep the wild beasts from leaping the railings and discommoding the audience.

Doors open at 7; performance begins at 8.

Positively no free list.

Diodorus Job Press.

Notwithstanding the inclemency of the weather, quite a respectable number of the rank and fashion of the city assembled last night to witness the debut upon metropolitan boards of the young tragedian who has of late been winning such golden opinions in the amphitheatres of the provinces. Some sixty thousand persons were present, and but for the fact that the streets were almost impassable, it is fair to presume that the house would have been full. His august Majesty, the Emperor Aurelius, occupied the imperial box, and was the cynosure of all eyes. Many illustrious nobles and generals of the Empire graced the occasion with their presence, and not the least among them was the young patrician lieutenant whose laurels, won in the ranks of the "Thundering Legion," are still so green upon his brow. The cheer which greeted his entrance was heard beyond the Tiber!

The late repairs and decorations add both to the comeliness and the comfort of the Coliseum. The new cushions are a great improvement upon the hard marble seats we have been so long accustomed to. The present management deserve well of the public. They have restored to the Coliseum the gilding, the rich upholstery and the uniform magnificence which old Coliseum frequenters tell us Rome was so proud of fifty years ago.

The opening scene last night--the broadsword combat between two young amateurs and a famous Parthian gladiator who was sent here a prisoner--was very fine. The elder of the two young gentlemen handled his weapon with a grace that marked the possession of extraordinary talent. His feint of thrusting, followed instantly by a happily delivered blow which unhelmeted the Parthian, was received with hearty applause. He was not thoroughly up in the backhanded stroke, but it was very gratifying to his numerous friends to know that, in time, practice would have overcome this defect. However, he was killed. His sisters, who were present, expressed considerable regret. His mother left the Coliseum. The other youth maintained the contest with such spirit as to call forth enthusiastic bursts of applause. When at last he fell a corpse, his aged mother ran screaming, with hair disheveled and tears streaming from her eyes, and swooned away just as her hands were clutching at the railings of the arena. She was promptly removed by the police. Under the circumstances the woman's conduct was pardonable, perhaps, but we suggest that such exhibitions interfere with the decorum which should be preserved during the performances, and are highly improper in the presence of the Emperor. The Parthian prisoner fought bravely and well; and well he might, for he was fighting for both life and liberty. His wife and children were there to nerve his arm with their love, and to remind him of the old home he should see again if he conquered. When his second assailant fell, the woman clasped her children to her breast and wept for joy. But it was only a transient happiness. The captive staggered toward her and she saw that the liberty he had earned was earned too late. He was wounded unto death. Thus the first act closed in a manner which was entirely satisfactory. The manager was called before the curtain and returned his thanks for the honor done him, in a speech which was replete with wit and humor, and closed by hoping that his humble efforts to afford cheerful and instructive entertainment would continue to meet with the approbation of the Roman public.

The star now appeared, and was received with vociferous applause and the simultaneous waving of sixty thousand handkerchiefs. Marcus Marcellus Valerian (stage name--his real name is Smith,) is a splendid specimen of physical development, and an artist of rare merit. His management of the battle-ax is wonderful. His gayety and his playfulness are irresistible, in his comic parts, and yet they are inferior to his sublime conceptions in the grave realm of tragedy. When his ax was describing fiery circles about the heads of the bewildered barbarians, in exact time with his springing body and his prancing legs, the audience gave way to uncontrollable bursts of laughter; but when the back of his weapon broke the skull of one and almost in the same instant its edge clove the other's body in twain, the howl of enthusiastic applause that shook the building, was the acknowledgment of a critical assemblage that he was a master of the noblest department of his profession. If he has a fault, (and we are sorry to even intimate that he has,) it is that of glancing at the audience, in the midst of the most exciting moments of the performance, as if seeking admiration. The pausing in a fight to bow when bouquets are thrown to him is also in bad taste. In the great left-handed combat he appeared to be looking at the audience half the time, instead of carving his adversaries; and when he had slain all the sophomores and was dallying with the freshman, he stooped and snatched a bouquet as it fell, and offered it to his adversary at a time when a blow was descending which promised favorably to be his death-warrant. Such levity is proper enough in the provinces, we make no doubt, but it ill suits the dignity of the metropolis. We trust our young friend will take these remarks in good part, for we mean them solely for his benefit. All who know us are aware that although we are at times justly severe upon tigers and martyrs, we never intentionally offend gladiators. The Infant Prodigy performed wonders. He overcame his four tiger whelps with ease, and with no other hurt than the loss of a portion of his scalp. The General Slaughter was rendered with a faithfulness to details which reflects the highest credit upon the late participants in it […]

A matinee for the little folks is promised for this afternoon, on which occasion several martyrs will be eaten by the tigers. The regular performance will continue every night till further notice. Material change of programme every evening. Benefit of Valerian, Tuesday, 29th, if he lives.

Mark Twain, *The Innocents Abroad, Or The New Pilgrim's Progress*, 1869

Sir Lawrence Alma-Tadema, *Preparation
in the Colosseum*, 1912, oil on canvas,
153.5 x 79.5 cm, private collection

It is the last painting of the artist which reworks,
isolating the extreme right portion of the previous
Caracalla and Geta, in a moment which this time
precedes the arrival of the public.

Edmund Blair Leighton, *The Gladiator's Wife*, 1884, oil on canvas, 155 x 94 cm, private collection

René Goscinny, Albert Uderzo,
The Adventures of Asterix the Gladiator,
12th March 1976

The presence of a Colosseum in the events in which
the Gallic warrior with his sidekick Obelix reaches
Rome, and is forced to fight on occasion of a great
show in honour of Julius Caesar is of course
anachronistic, could instead portray a generic
amphitheatre. Instead a surreal setting forms the
context of the futuristic stories of the cartoon
Ranxerox, created in 1978 by Tamburini and
Liberatore, whose protagonist is a negative yet
immortal hero, as a result of being assembled from
pieces of photocopying. In one episode he finds
himself "abandoned near the Colosseum, completely
disabled, with a timed remote control in his cerebral
circuits". The building became a reinforced concrete
hotel, although originally it was to be remade in pink
plexiglas.

A selection of frames from *Gladiators of Rome*, directed by Iginio Straffi, the creator of Winx, the first 3D animation film on the genre (Italy, 2012)

Two frames from 2013's videogame *Ryse: Son of Rome*, in which one has the ability to fight, in single or multiplayer, in the role of a gladiator in the Colosseum

The Colosseum, between past and present, is at the heart of the grim events of two chapters of the successful *Assassin's Creed* series, 2010's *Brotherhood* and 2014's *Identity*, set in the Renaissance in which one engages in a struggle against the excessive power of the Borgia family, to liberate the monument from decay and begin its restoration. The area around the arena is fairly faithfully rendered, which reflects contemporary and successful views.

The tradition of modern centurions stationed around
the Colosseum represents a daily attraction for prime
Selfies for tourists.

Parade of historical re-enactment groups,
Rome, Colosseum, 19th April 2015

Within the Colosseum the echo of the struggles of gladiators still resonates, and the courage of their broken lives. That extreme energy which takes hold of the dance. It suggests new frontiers to overcome.

Valeria Crippa

With the partial reconstruction of the arena floor, the amphitheatre returned to hosting performances, even during the evening with atmospheric lighting, of the classical tragedies, such as *Oedipus Rex* in Ancient Greek, and an experimental production of the Senecan Medea. Yet it has also, for a select audience, hosted concerts of international stars such as Paul McCartney in 2003, Andrea Bocelli, Ray Charles and then Biagio Antonacci, who recorded a live music album, *Colosseo*. Dance events too, have been welcomed at the Colosseum, such as *Roberto Bolle and Friends*. Many more artists have played and sung outside.

Roberto Bolle, in *L'Arlesienne* by Roland
Petit, Colosseum, 2008, photograph by
Luciano Romano

The Christian Colosseum

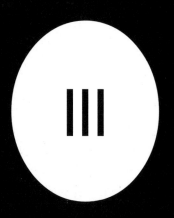

The vision that the Spanish artist José Benlliure y Gil gives is indeed apocalyptic, with theatrical light in the thirty five square metres of his canvas from the Prado, *El último martir,* dated to 1885. Within the Colosseum, reduced to a spectral skeleton, the crowds appear gathered around San Almáquio, raising the cross to end the gladiatorial games and liberate the multitude from their guilt.

Even if there is no reliable evidence of Christians slaughtered in the Colosseum, it is possible that those who were martyred in Rome, met their deaths in the deplorable practice of *damnatio ad bestias,* which consisted in the public execution of criminals and prisoners, destined to be devoured by beasts, brought in great quantities from exotic lands for use in the shows, to supply *venationes* and extravagant duels be tween animals. In his *Letters to the Romans*, Saint Ignatius Bishop of Antioch at the beginning of the 2nd century AD, one of the first to voluntarily offer himself for condemnation to the wild beasts rather than deny the faith, offers a different per spective on the amphitheatre, one which from the point o view of the victims is chilling. Thanks to the emphasis place on cruelty towards the innocent made to suffer in the arena the image of the martyr diffused among the first Christia communities as an instrument of salvation for the believers and soon became an key weapon of the Fathers of the Churc against pagans and the Roman authorities, taking advantag of the seductive attraction of the games, as indeed did the Emperors.

While in the medieval imagination the mass of th amphitheatre, having lost its original function and suffered th ravages of time, imposed itself threateningly on the urba landscape like a theatre of the persistence of the dark paga gods, a space in which necromancy was practised and whic was as a new Tower of Babel. However, the presence of di ferent cult sites around the body of the Colosseum in realit made it a Christian monument: among the churches of Sa Salvatore *de Rota Colisei* and *San Nicola del Colosseo,* th

... use by the powerful confraternity of the Santissimo Salvatore al Sancta Sanctorum – of which the emblem with the face of Christ sculpted on the keystone of the central and eastern archway of the building remains – which during the Avignon captivity conducted the vital tasks of assistance and care. The ruins of the amphitheatre with wooden shacks clinging to the perimeter structures by the sloping roofs, which left marks on the surface as a result of having been strongly fixed to the ground, provided an ideal setting for sacred scenes. In the *Adoration of the Magi*, of the Dutch Breenbergh, for instance the ruins appear to be paced in a vision of open countryside.

The Colosseum of the time appears in various scenes of martyrdom which were perpetrated in the area. The most commonly represented, especially from the fifteenth century onwards - when a high concentration of these type of iconography appears along with copious quantities of artistic studies of the amphitheatre as an architectural model - is naturally that of Saint Sebastian (Pinturicchio, Signorelli, the Frenchman Josse Lieferinxe etc.), but also in those of Saint Peter, Saint Bibiana and Saint Serapia it appears in the distance, as a topographical landmark of the city.

Drawings, paintings, engravings and then photographs repeatedly show the numerous transformations which over time have characterised the Christianisation of the structure (in an age of reaffirmation of the church as promoted by the Counter Reformation), from just about every angle; by day at sunset and by moonlight. Escaping systematic destruction Pius V eventually inserted the Colosseum into the route for pilgrims, for whom was prescribed the gathering of earth from the arena, as a kind of relic, steeped as it was in the blood of martyrs. Meanwhile, already by 1519 the Chapel of Santa Maria della Pietà had been built with the very stones of the Colosseum, as the basis for the rite of the Passion of Christ, then after decades of neglect it was reopened to the cult in 1622 and bestowed with a bell tower and entrusted to the care of a succession of hermits. Yet the first consecration of the site had to wait for Clement X, beginning with the erection of a ...

wooden cross on the summit of the monument on the occasion of the 1675 Jubilee. This was followed, under Clement XI, by a commission given to Carlo Fontana to conduct a comprehensive restoration of the Flavian Amphitheatre, which conceived the construction of a sanctuary dedicated to the martyrs within the arena. The failure of this ambitious project was remedied by placing a Cross in the centre of the area. A Cross – "kissed from morning until night", in the words of Dickens – remaining in its place for the almost two centuries in which it formed part of an itinerary, which included collective Mass and Communion, to earn an indulgence. The mute witnesses which were the aediculae of the Via Crucis, erected along the perimeter of the arena, temporarily removed and then re-erected for the final consecration in 1749 by Benedict XIV in view of the 1750 Jubilee, damaged during the Napoleonic occupation, restored and then dismantled for good in 1874, when the excavations brought the hypogeum to light. Pietro Rosa, however, kept most of the architectural elements: this makes their reconstruction still possible. Their spiritual presence comes to life again in the celebrations of Good Friday, when the Popes proceed at night, station by station, between the praying crowds on an evocative route through the monument.

José Benlliure y Gil, *The Vision in the Colosseum. The Last Martyr*, 1885, oil on canvas, 561 x 728 cm, Valencia, in storage from Museo del Prado

The Christian Colosseum

Riflessione immorale sur Culiseo

St'arcate rotte c'oggi li pittori
Viengheno a ddiseggnà cco li pennelli,
Tra ll'arberetti, le crosce, li fiori,
Le farfalle e li canti de l'uscelli,

A ttempo de l'antichi imperatori
Ereno un fiteatro, indove quelli
Curreveno a vvedé li gradiatori
Sfracassasse le coste e li scervelli.

Cqua llòro se pijjaveno piascere
De sentì ll'urli de tanti cristiani
Carpestati e sbranati da le fiere.

Allora tante stragge e ttanto lutto,
E adesso tanta pasce! Oh avventi umani!
Cos'è sto monno! Come cammia tutto!

Giuseppe Gioachino Belli, *Sonetti*, 4th September 1835

The Christian Colosseum

Herbert Gustave Schmalz, *Faithful Unto Death. Christians to the Lions!*, c.1888, oil on canvas, 165 x 114 cm, private collection

Agostino Caironi, *Family of Early Christians about to be Devoured by Wild Beasts*, 1852, oil on canvas, 236 x 175 cm, Milan, Accademia di Belle Arti di Brera, Quadreria

The Christian Colosseum

François-Léon Benouville, *Christian Martyrs going into the Amphitheatre*, 1855, oil on canvas, 459 x 391 cm, Paris, Musée d'Orsay

[…] Perhaps there are few persons who will notice this plant (the Paliurus, or Jerusalem thorn) flourishing upon the vast ruins of the Colosseum of Rome, without being moved to reflect upon the scenes that have taken place on the ground on which he stands, and remember the numbers of those holy men who bore witness to the truth of their belief in Jesus and shed their blood before the thousands of Pagans assembled around, as a testimony, securing for themselves an eternal crown, without thorns, and to us those blessed truths, on which only we build our future hope of bliss, and derive our present peace and comfort.

Richard Deakin, *Flora of the Colosseum of Rome*, 1855

The Christian Colosseum

Jean-Léon Gérôme, *The Christian Martyrs'*
Last Prayer, 1863-1883, oil on canvas,
87.9 x 150.1 cm, Baltimore, The Walters
Art Museum

This masterpiece, focused on the persecution of Christians by Nero after 64 AD, underwent a lengthy development with several changes, not so much in terms of the faithfulness of representation, on which the artist allowed himself various liberties – the Circus Maximus became a distorted Colosseum to give panoramic breadth to the scene – but on the intensity of the portrayal. Some drafts held at Nancy attest to the attention the artist dedicated to the figures of the martyrs hoisted on poles to become many human torches, such as in the celebrated painting by Siemiradzki, and to the group of Christians gathered around the Master, a modern Socrates who is proud to face the end which he will meet. The gathered martyrs are innocent in their clothing and delicate colours, and studied in their gestures and expressions despite being far from the viewer and smaller than the fierce lion which

dominates both the foreground and indeed painting, almost as a signature of the artist to whose name it was alluding. The lion's entrance into the arena, almost as a superstar, has a cinematic flavour to it, because it suggests, like the trails marked in the sand, an action: other lions and tigers follow to invade the arena without salvation. This is clearly evident in a later painting by the artist, the 1902 *Gathering Up the Lions in the Circus*, where the beasts are driven back by force into the underground vaults, while the stands of the arena empty, and the floor is littered with pools of blood and the chillingly mangled remains of Christians, with a horror worthy of the latest pulp fiction. These paintings were to inspire, like a *tableau vivant*, Enrico Guazzoni in his 1913 adaptation of the novel *Quo Vadis?* whose pages Gérôme had masterfully translated into painting.

Some accounts make these the prisons of the wild beasts destined for the amphitheatre; some the prisons of the condemned gladiators; some, both. But the legend most appalling to the fancy is, that in the upper range (for there are two stories of these caves) the Early Christians destined to be eaten at the Coliseum Shows, heard the wild beasts, hungry for them, roaring down below; until, upon the night and solitude of their captivity, there burst the sudden noon and life of the vast theatre crowded to the parapet, and of these, their dreaded neighbours, bounding in!

Charles Dickens, *Pictures from Italy*, 1846

The Christian Colosseum

Jean-Léon Gérôme, *Gathering Up the Lions in the Circus*, 1902, oil on canvas, 82 x 130 cm, private collection

Henryk H. Siemiradzki, *The Future
Victims of the Colosseum*, total and detail,
1899, oil on canvas, 198.5 x 142 cm,
Warsaw, Bishop's Seminary

　　　　　　　　　　　　　The Christian Colosseum

While a group of people are listening to a spiritual
lesson of one of the followers of Peter or Paul, the
sunlight illuminates the Colosseum in the
background, from which the colossal gilded bronze
statue of Nero as the Sun God (radiant head,
Victoria on the right hand) appears, which itself was
the masterpiece of Zenodorus and gave its name to
the amphitheatre. To paint the colossus, in its
secondary Hadrianic positioning closer to the
building, the Polish painter for whom Italy was a
second home and who was a friend of the writer
Sienkiewicz, did not limit himself to reading
Suetonius or Pliny the Elder, but had analysed the
iconographic sources, including ancient coinage such
as that of Gordian III, and the most recent
nineteenth century reconstructions by young
architects, guests of the French Academy of Villa
Medici.

Summoned before Trajan… for his refusal to honour the gods, St. Ignatius met the accusation by eloquently denouncing the follies of paganism. He was brought to Rome to be put to death with criminals in the amphitheatre. He listened to the verdict with joy, aided with his own hands of those who chained him, and set out on the long journey as one who returns to his homeland.

On his arrival he was handed over to the Urban Prefect, and had a moment to breathe until the recurrence of a celebrated festival with the usual shows in the amphitheatre. Led into the arena he kneeled and exclaimed in a loud voice: "Romans present in this place for no crime, yet here so that I may yet thus enjoy the glory of God, for whose sake I have been imprisoned. I am the seed of His field and I must be buried by the fangs of the lions to deserve to be transformed into bread for His table".

At this point the lions were released, and at once devoured him, leaving nothing of his body, save the greater bones, which the Christians by night could gather so that they might bury them.

Charles Isadore Hemans, *The Story of Monuments in Rome and her Environs*, 1864

The Christian Colosseum

A miniature of the celebrated *Menologion of Basil II*, dating to the late 10th century and preserved in the Biblioteca Apostolica Vaticana, depicting the martyrdom of St. Ignatius, the Bishop of Antioch of the 2nd century AD who was, according to tradition, the first Christian martyr of the Colosseum.

S. Meyrick-Jones, cartoon appearing on the number of the weekly "The Spectator" of the 18th November 2000 in which even British humour is exercised on the Christian/Lions *topos*: "You're right, I was a fool to give in to those damned animal rights activists!"

Anonymous Fabriczy, *The Colosseum with the Church of San Giacomo*, 1568-1572, Stuttgart, Staatgalerie

Circle of Bartholomeus Breenbergh,
Adoration of the Magi, c.1640-1650,
oil on copper, 29 x 49 cm, Amsterdam,
Rijksmuseum

Pinturicchio, *The Martyrdom of Saint Sebastian*, 1492-1494, fresco, Vatican City, Vatican Museums, Borgia Apartments

The Christian Colosseum

Luca Signorelli, *The Martyrdom of Saint Sebastian*, 1498, tempera on panel, 288 x 175 cm, Città di Castello, Pinacoteca Comunale

97

After the unrealised proposal of Gian Lorenzo
Bernini to construct a chapel at the centre of the
arena "where earlier there lay an altar upon which
were laid sacrifices to Jupiter", in 1696 one of his
students, Carlo Fontana, conceived the plan - which
was also to remain unrealised - of a sanctuary
dedicated to the Christian martyrs with a
monumental temple in the centre, situated on the
major axis and surrounded by a porticoed perimeter.

The Christian Colosseum

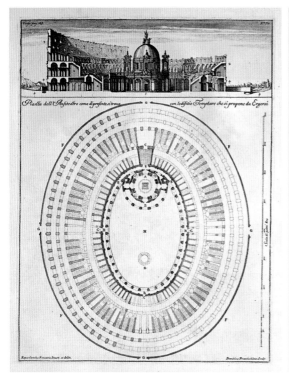

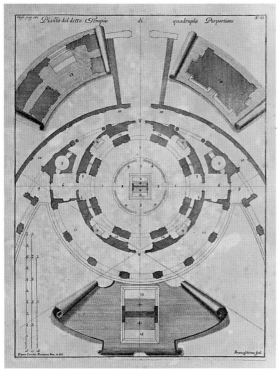

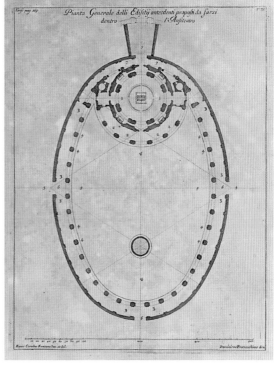

Carlo Fontana, Plan for a church in the
Colosseum, symbol of the "Ecclesia
Triumphans", by C. Fontana, *L'Anfiteatro
Flavio descritto e delineato dal Caval. Carlo
Fontana diviso in libri sei*, L'Aja 1725

The signature of the French artist Hubert
Robert inscribed on a pillar of the
ambulacrum of the I order of the
amphitheatre, 1762

The Parisian artist's predilection for the Colosseum is
borne witness to in paintings and drawings: it was a
sort of existential identification, a place of imagination
and memory. By now close to departing after a long
stay in Rome - the date inscribed under the 'signature'
is 1762 - Robert leaves his name on the 'living flesh'
of the Colosseum, in epigraphic letters worthy of an
ancient inscription: inserting himself, in an indelible
way, in the history of the monument and Rome
(Serena Romano).

The painting, of which there is also another version,
faithfully portrays the type of use of the ground floor
of the Colosseum at the end of the eighteenth
century, according to ways already firmly rooted in the
late Medieval Era: the perimeter gallery was divided
into areas by walls built with recycled material, closed
by wooden doors and with minimal furnishings
between which we see an ancient sarcophagus that
remains in the amphitheatre even today. On the right
we see a lady, arranging flowers in the large pitcher,
gesturing at her companion not to disturb the
mediation of the monk who is concentrated on
reading the sacred texts. (Rossella Rea).

The Christian Colosseum

Hubert Robert, *Hermit in the Colosseum*,
oil on canvas, 18th century, private
collection

Anne Louis Girodet de Roucy Trioson,
Portrait of François-René de Chateaubriand,
1809, oil on canvas, 120 x 96 cm,
Saint-Malo, Musée d'Histoire de la Ville
et du Pays Malouin

The Christian Colosseum

One beautiful evening, last July, I was sitting in the Coliseum, on the step of an altar dedicated to the sufferings of the Passion. The setting sun poured floods of gold through all the galleries, where crowds had once thronged; at the same time, strong shadows emerged from the recesses of the ruined room and corridors, or fell to the ground in large black stripes. From the heights of the structure, I perceived, between the ruins, on the right of the edifice, the gardens of the palace of the Caesars, with a palm-tree, which seemed to have been placed in the midst of this wreck expressly for painters and poets. In this amphitheatre, instead of the shouts of joy from ferocious spectators watching Christians being torn apart by lions, nothing was now heard but the barking of dogs, which belong to the hermit who guards the ruins. But as soon as the sun fell below the horizon, the clock in the dome of Saint Peter's resounded through the porticoes of the Coliseum. This correspondence, established by sacred sounds, between the two grandest monuments of Pagan and Christian Rome, invoked a lively emotion; I reflected that the modern edifice would fall as the ancient one had; that monuments succeed each other like the men who erected them […]. The vaulted roofs that now re-echoed to the sound of this Christian bell were the work of a Pagan emperor, designated by prophecy to complete the final destruction of Jerusalem. Are not these sufficiently exalted, subjects of meditation, and do you not think that a city where such effects are to be produced at every step is worthy of being viewed?

Yesterday, the 9th of January, I returned to the Coliseum, to see it at another season, in another aspect; I was surprised, on arrival, not to hear the dogs, which generally appeared in the upper corridors of the amphitheatre, barking among the withered grass. I knocked at the door of the hermitage, built beneath one of the arches; no one replied; the hermit was dead. The inclemency of the season, the absence of that worthy recluse, combined with several troubling recollections, redoubled the melancholy inspired by the place; I almost supposed myself looking at the ruins of a building which I had, a few days before, admired in all its newness and perfection! It is thus […] that we are constantly reminded of our nothingness; Human beings search outside themselves for reasons to be convinced; they meditate on the ruins of empires, forgetting that they are ruins yet more unstable, which will perish before these relics do.

François Auguste René de Chateaubriand, *Travels in Italy*, 1803-1804

The Christian Colosseum

The eighteenth century engraving, concerns a
drawing from the school of Pannini, documents a
moment in the life of the amphitheatre which
was near the consecration of the arena to the
Passion of Christ in 1749, and the construction
of the aedicules of the Via Crucis

William Pars, *The Interior of the Colosseum*,
c.1775, watercolour, ink and graphite on
paper, 435 x 591 mm, London, Tate

In the bird's eye view of the Colosseum,
engraved by Giovanni Battista in 1776
(etching, 53.7 x 78 cm), one sees the 14
aedicules of the Stations of the Cross around
the arena, and at the centre the great cross

The Christian Colosseum

Christoffer Wilhelm Eckersberg,
The Interior of the Colosseum, 1813-1816,
oil on canvas, 32 x 25.5 cm, Copenhagen,
Thorvaldsen Museum

The Danish painter, author of numerous views of the
Colosseum during his travels in Italy, was struck by
the scene of religious life which was played out
before the Chapel of Santa Maria della Pietà.

107

The Christian Colosseum

In the work of the largest format ever produced by a lover of the Colosseum, such as that painted by Granet in the first years of his presence in Rome, the painter invites us to mediate in silence, just as the humble devotees in prayer before the Chapel, on the only expression of the white light. He remains in shadows as if to apologise for taking on so grandiose a subject. Choosing the main entrance, he keeps to one side under the access arch: the monument, in his perspective more ruined as it was before the Napoleonic restorations, does not then appear within this frame, a painting within a painting, with its own "windows" which allow the gaze to escape into the distance. To be at the Colosseum for sure, to paint it yes, but at the same time he hides it (Denis Coutagne).

François-Marius Granet, *Interior View of the Colosseum*, 1804, oil on canvas, 125 x 160 cm, Paris, Musée del Louvre

Sylvester Shchedrin, *The Colosseum*, 1819,
oil on canvas, 62.5 x 48.7 cm, Moscow,
State Tretyakov Gallery

Hébert added that, if necessary, one could even sleep among the ruins of the Colosseum… since the benefits of the "historical shivers" it gave were worth the risk of catching a cold.

Claude Debussy, *Monsieur Croche the Dilettante Hater*

Ernest Antoine Auguste Hébert, Rome,
*Interior of the Colosseum and Way of the Cross
of Good Friday*, 19th century, oil on canvas,
80 x 115 cm, Paris, Musée Ernest Hébert

Rome, 2nd April 1874

The excavations in the Colosseum proceed apace; huge subterranean canals are brought to light. Nothing important in the way of statues has been discovered. In order to make these excavations, all the chapels of the Stations and also the Cross in the middle have been removed. This proceeding aroused a storm on the part of all the pious and in the Vatican. The Cardinal Vicar laid the Director Rosa under the ban; processions daily wound their way to the Colosseum to pray. Digging was industriously carried on.

Gregorovius, *The Roman Journals*, 1852-1874

Gioacchino Altobelli, *Interior of the
Colosseum by Moonlight*, c.1865, albumen
print, 29.3 x 38 cm, Paris, Musée d'Orsay

John Paul II presides over the Stations of the Cross at the Colosseum, Rome, 29th March 2002

The Christian Colosseum

Interior of the Colosseum with the Cross
lit, on occasion of the Good Friday
procession, Rome, 3rd April 2015

By Moonlight, Posing for the Grand Tour

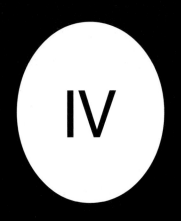

IV

Generation after generation of painters, the whole dazzling length of the list of them, was seduced by the landscapes of the ruins of Ancient Rome, producing hundreds upon hundreds of drawings, watercolours and paintings in which the Colosseum stands out among other monuments for its sheer size. The subject, much debated by art historians, nevertheless continues to result in new discoveries because, as Ernst H. Gombrich argued: "Every time that we put ourselves before them, the great works appear different. They seem both inexhaustible and unpredictable, like real human beings".

This place, full of arches and alleys and besieged by vegetation, becomes the prototype of unsettling ruins for Flemish and Dutch artists. Van Heemskerck, who nevertheless celebrated himself and his activities as a painter in the manner of humanism by painting himself before the amphitheatre at the time, which in other works he transformed into a silver platform for games. Pieter Breughel turned into a Tower of Babel, then symbol of human madness which permeated the society as well as the religious and political culture of the time.

After having made an appearance in the background behind martyrs and more or less mythical stories on Italian panels and frescoes, the unmistakeable outline of the Colosseum is already isolated as a view at the beginning of the 16th century, in the perspective tricks of the wood inlays of the choir of the Abbey of Monte Oliveto Maggiore, and in the frieze of the Hall of Eagles of the Palazzo dei Conservatori on the Capitoline Hill, where, under Paul III Farnese, Cristoforo Gerard demonstrated a theory of urban landscapes, often built around famous monuments. The classicism of Lorraine – with lyrical abandon of his mythical landscapes, imbued with a golden and suffused light, where the ancient buildings are framed by soft natural scenes which follow one another according to studied effects of depth – pervade the many, warmer bucolic scenes, such as those of Van Bloemen, which, between the 17th and 18th centuries, restored the Colosseum to a solemn sacredness, in a harmonious collection where the poetry of nature and myth discover the tenets of a perfect equilibrium.

Yet throughout the 19th century, Italy was the destina

...ion of the young Northern European elite gentleman, but also Russian and American, who carried out his journey towards the South as a rite of passage, an essential step of their education. He aspired to be immortalised in elegant portraits, also for couples or groups in this new, exclusive cultural habitat in the shadow of the Colosseum. A visit to the Colosseum itself was an unmissable experience in the eyes of writers, who held it worthwhile to brave the dangers due to the precarious safety conditions of the monument.

Among them, artists and writers especially found it hard to leave Rome for years and whole decades, captivated by that nostalgia for the Ancient, which manifested in a continuous homage and indescribable admiration towards the Colosseum: the choice of images and words intertwined in the following pages serve to evoke a similarly fruitful inspiration.

The Colosseum had meanwhile become an *amphithearum naturae,* a sort of wild botanical garden, where mosses and twigs grew; branches and vines hung from the vaults as in a jungle, and the light filtered between the leaves. Botanists soon learned of this bizarre microclimate, and recorded it in their treatises, and with the prevalence of romantic sensitivity over the purely archaeological interests, the vegetal metamorphoses of the monument fascinated painters (Ducros, von Alt, Townley and many others) who in their paintings knew how to evoke this strange and enchanting effect. French painters especially, such as Costantin and his student Granet, portrayed the Colosseum by moonlight, with overgrown grottos and arches crowned with blades of grass and flowers from which the sky sprung. The lights and shadows rendered the distinction between ancient and new ambiguous, transforming the stone into a place of imagination. Escher too seems to have been an heir, in the '30s, of the glorious tradition of the nineteenth century *vedutisti* in their nocturnal views of the amphitheatre, depicted from the outside by the colourful, material results of artists such as Oscar Kokoschka, Achille Funi (*The Colosseum*, 1930, Rome, Galleria Comunale d'Arte Moderna e Contemporanea), Mario Mafai (*Colosseum*, 1965, Rovereto, MaRT) just before the outline of the building became a pop icon.

Gaspar van Wittel, *The Colosseum and the Arch of Constantine*, 1730's, oil on canvas, 25.5 x 47 cm, Antichità Alberto Di Castro

Thomas Hiram Hotchkiss, *View of the Colosseum at Sunset*, 1865, oil on paper, Collection of the New-York Historical Society

Marten van Heemskerck, *Self-Portrait with the
Colosseum*, 1553, oil on panel, 42.2 x 56.5 cm,
Cambridge, Fitzwilliam Museum.

Marten van Heemskerck, *Imaginary view
of an Ancient Area (Running of the bulls
in the Colosseum)*, 1552, oil on panel,
73.5 x 121 cm, Lille, Palais des Beaux Arts

By Moonlight, Posing for the Grand Tour

Pieter Bruegel the Elder, *The Tower of Babel*, 1563, oil on panel, 114 x 155 cm, Vienna, Kunsthistorisches Museum.

The huge tower was erected so as to invoke the architectural structures of the Colosseum, the ruins of which were known to the Flemish painter from prints, and from having observed it from life during his visit to Italy: he was in Rome in 1533 as a guest of the miniaturist Giulio Clovio. The technical details of the construction indeed reveal an uncommon competence in the field of building. The inspiration of the Colosseum is after all coherent with the allegorical meaning of the painting: the amphitheatre was indeed the site of the martyrdom of Christians, the perfect symbol of the challenge to God of the Roman Emperors.

By Moonlight, Posing for the Grand Tour

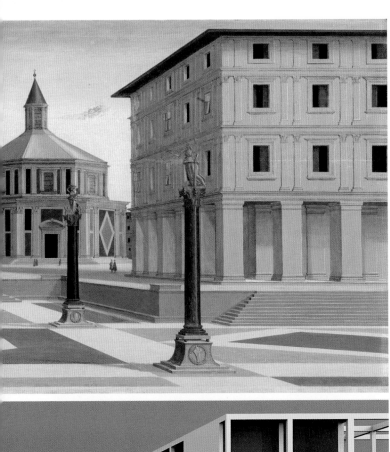

Central Italian Painter, *Ideal City*, 1480-1490?, tempera on panel, 80.3 x 219.8 cm, Baltimore, The Walters Art Gallery

Victor Burgin, *The Ideal City*, 2014

123

Fra Giovanni da Verona, Wood inlay with a view
of the Colosseum, 1503-1505, Asciano (SI),
Abbey of Monte Oliveto Maggiore, choir

By Moonlight, Posing for the Grand Tour

Cristoforo Gherardi, *The Colosseum*, from
the frescoed frieze of the Hall of the
Eagles within Palazzo dei Conservatori,
Rome, mid 16th century

Jan Frans van Bloemen called Orizzonte,
*View of the Palatine, the Arch of Constantine
and the Colosseum from Caelian Hill,*
c.1740, oil on canvas, 74 x 151 cm, Rome,
Accademia Nazionale di San Luca

Rome, 11th November 1786

In the evening we came upon the Coliseum, when it was already twilight. When one looks at it, all else seems little; the edifice is so vast, that one can not hold the image of it in one's soul—in memory we think it smaller, and then return to it again to find it every time greater than before.

Johann Wolfgang Goethe, *Italian Journey*, 1787

By Moonlight, Posing for the Grand Tour

Jacob-Philipp Hackert, *Johann Wolfgang Goethe visiting the Colosseum in Rome*, c.1790, oil on canvas, Rome, Casa di Goethe

Rome, 2nd February 1787 – Of the beauty of a walk through Rome by moonlight it is impossible to form a conception, without having witnessed it. All single objects are swallowed up by the great masses of light and shade, and nothing but grand and general outlines present themselves to the eye. For three several days we have enjoyed to the full the brightest and most glorious of nights. Peculiarly beautiful at such a time is the Coliseum. At night it is always closed; a hermit dwells in a little shrine within its range, and beggars of all kinds nestle beneath its crumbling arches; the latter had lit a fire on the arena, and a gentle wind bore down the smoke to the ground, so that the lower portion of the ruins was quite hid by it, while above the vast walls stood out in deeper darkness before the eye. As we stopt at the gate to contemplate the scene through the iron gratings, the moon shone brightly in the heavens above. Presently the smoke found its way up the sides, and through every chink and opening, while the moon lit it up like a cloud. The sight was exceedingly glorious.

Johann Wolfgang Goethe, *Italian Journey*, 1787

Bernardo Bellotto, *Capriccio with Colosseum*, 1746, oil on canvas, 132.5 x 117 cm, Parma, Galleria Nazionale

The night before her departure, unable to sleep, she heard a troop of Romans singing in the moonlight. She could not resist her desire to follow them, and once more wander through that beloved scene. She dressed [...] and bidding her servants keep the carriage within sight of her, put on a veil, to avoid recognition, and, at some distance, pursued the musicians [...]. At last the singers departed, and left Corinne near the Coliseum: she wished to enter its enclosure and bid adieu to ancient Rome. Those who have seen this place but by day cannot judge of the impression it may make. The sun of Italy should shine on festivals; but the moon is the light for ruins. Sometimes, through the openings of the amphitheatre, which seems towering to the clouds, a portion of heaven's vault appears like a dark blue curtain. The plants that cling to the broken walls all wear the hues of night. The soul at once shudders and melts on finding itself alone with nature. One side of this edifice is much more fallen than the other: the two contemporaries make an unequal struggle against time. He fells the weakest; the other still resists, but soon must yield.

Madame De Staël, *Corinne or Italy*, 1807

Carl Gustav Carus, *View of the Colosseum by Night*, c.1830, 48 x 37 cm, Saint Petersburg, State Hermitage Museum

MANFRED (*alone*)

The stars are forth, the moon above the tops
Of the snow-shining mountains.– Beautiful!
I linger yet with Nature, for the night
Hath been to me a more familiar face
Than that of man; and in her starry shade
Of dim, and solitary loveliness,
I learn'd the language of another world.
I do remember me, that in my youth,
When I was wandering,– upon such a night
I stood within the Colosseum's wall,
Midst the chief relics of almighty Rome.
The trees which grew along the broken arches
Waved dark in the blue midnight, and the stars
Shone through the rents of ruin; from afar
The watchdog bay'd beyond the Tiber; and
More near from out the Caesars' palace came
The owl's long cry, and, interruptedly,
Of distant sentinels the fitful song
Begun and died upon the gentle wind.
Some cypresses beyond the time-worn breach
Appear'd to skirt the horizon, yet they stood
Within a bowshot. Where the Caesars dwelt,
And dwell the tuneless birds of night, amidst
A grove which springs through levell'd battlements,
And twines its roots with the imperial hearths,
Ivy usurps the laurel's place of growth;–
But the gladiators' bloody Circus stands,
A noble wreck in ruinous perfection!
While Caesar's chambers, and the Augustan halls
Grovel on earth in indistinct decay.–
And thou didst shine, thou rolling moon, upon
All this, and cast a wide and tender light,
Which soften'd down the hoar austerity
Of rugged desolation, and fill'd up,
As 'twere anew, the gaps of centuries;
Leaving that beautiful which still was so,
And making that which was not, till the place
Became religion, and the heart ran o'er
With silent worship of the great of old,–
The dead, but sceptred sovereigns, who still rule
Our spirits from their urns.–
      'Twas such a night!
'Tis strange that I recall it at this time;
But I have found our thoughts take wildest flight
Even at the moment when they should array
Themselves in pensive order.

George Gordon Byron, *Manfred*, 1817

      By Moonlight, Posing for the Grand Tour

James Tibitts-Willmore, *Lord George Byron contemplating the Colosseum*, engraving, 19th century, Paris, Bibliothèque des Arts Décoratifs

16th August 1827 – The Colosseum can be seen from three or four wholly different points of view. The finest perhaps is that which is offered to the spectator when he is in the arena where the gladiators fought, and he sees those immense ruins rise all about him. What impresses me most about it is that pure blue sky that one perceives through the upper openings of the building toward the north.

It is best to be alone in the Colosseum. Often you are annoyed by the pious murmurs of the devout who, in flocks of fifteen or twenty, make the stations of the cross, or by a Capuchin friar who, since Benedict XIV, who restored this edifice [...]

One climbs to the passageways of the upper stories by stairs that are in a fair state of repair. But if you are without a guide (and in Rome any cicerone is bound to spoil your pleasure), you run the risk of passing over vaults worn this by rain, that may collapse [...] From the height of the ruins of the Colosseum one lives simultaneously with Vespasian who built it, with St. Paul, with Michelangelo. Vespasian, triumphing over the Jews, once passed on the Via Sacra, near that arch of triumph erected to his son Titus, which, even in our day, the Jew avoids in his course. Here, closer by, is the Arch of Constantine; but it was built by architects who were already barbarians; decadence was beginning for Rome and the West.

I feel only too keenly that such sensations can be indicated, but cannot be communicated. Elsewhere these memories could be commonplace; for the traveler standing on these ruins, they are immense and full of emotion [...]

I would ask the reader who has not been to Rome to be good enough to glance at a picture of the Colosseum (that of Leseur, for example), or at least the illustration that is in the *Encyclopédie*.

You see an oval theatre, of enormous height, still entire on the exterior on the north side, but ruined toward the south. It could hold 107,000 spectators [...] There is nothing in the world so grandiose.

Stendhal, *A Roman Journal*, 1829

Thomas Cole, *Interior of the Colosseum in
Rome*, 1832, oil on canvas, 10 x 18 cm,
Albany Institute of History & Art
Purchase, Evelyn Newman Fund

30th May 1828 – […] Some days ago an Englishman arrived in Rome with his horses, which have brought him all the way from England. He refused a cicerone, and despite the sentinel's efforts he entered the Colosseum on horseback. Some hundred masons and galley slaves are constantly working to consolidate some wall that is crumbling from exposure to weather. The Englishman watched them work, and he told us that evening, "Begad! the Colosseum is the finest thing I've seen in Rome. I like that building. it will be magnificent when they have finished it." He though those men were building the Colosseum.

Stendhal, *A Roman Journal*, 1829

By Moonlight, Posing for the Grand Tour

Ippolito Caffi, *The Interior of the Colosseum*,
1857, oil on paper applied to canvas,
33.5 x 47.5 cm, Rome, Museo di Roma

The paintings which Caffi dedicated to the
Colosseum, including the splendid lunar one, reveal
the innovative perspectival research begun by the
artist in harmony with that of contemporary
photography. If on the one hand, the views of the
Colosseum suffer a certain standardisation,
positioning themselves as easily commercialised
souvenirs for an ever expanding public, on the other
the comparison with some calotypes can make one
hypothesise that Caffi frequented the environment
of painters/photographers who would give birth to
the "Roman School of Photography" who met at
Caffè Greco, where the artist had decorated certain
rooms with view of Venice and Rome. In particular,
this work merits a significant comparison with the
studies of Giacomo Caneva, which he had executed
a few years earlier, including some calotype s of the
Colosseum, setting it in a similar perspective to that
used by Caffi for these paintings (Federica Pirani).

140   By Moonlight, Posing for the Grand Tour

Ippolito Caffi, *Interior of the Colosseum from Above*, 1855, oil on paper applied to canvas, 56 x 90 cm, Rome, Museo di Roma

Er Culiseo

Quest'era pe la giostra e li fochetti
come se fa oggiggiorno da Corèa.
C'ereno attorno qui tutti parchetti,
lassù er loggiato, e immezzo la pratea.

Eppoi fatte inzegnà da mastr'Andrea
er butteghin de chiave e de bijetti,
er caffè pe gelati e limonea,
e scale, e rimessini, e trabocchetti.

Oh, la viacruce l'hanno messa doppo,
perché li Santi Martiri qui spesso
c'ebbero da ingozzà certo sciroppo.

Co un po' de sassi e un po' de carcia e gesso,
lassa che je se dii quarche arittoppo
e un'imbiancata, e po' servì anch'adesso.

Giuseppe Gioachino Belli, *Sonetti*, 4th October 1831

Louis Jean Desprez, *Interior of the Colosseum*, 18th century, watercolour and pen drawing, Palaiseau, École Polytechnique

Type of the antique Rome! Rich reliquary
Of lofty contemplation left to Time
By buried centuries of pomp and power!
At length, at length, after so many days
Of weary pilgrimage and burning thirst
(Thirst for the springs of lore that in thee lie),
I kneel, an altered and an humble man,
Amid thy shadows, and so drink within
My very soul thy grandeur, gloom, and glory!

Vastness, and age, and memories of eld!
Silence, and desolation, and dim night!
I feel ye now,—I feel ye in your strength.
[…]

Here, where a hero fell, a column falls!
Here, where the mimic eagle glared in gold,
A midnight vigil holds the swarthy bat!
Here, where the dames of Rome their gilded hair
Waved to the wind, now wave the reed and thistle!
Here, where on golden throne the monarch lolled,
Glides, spectre-like, unto his marble home,
Lit by the wan light of the horned moon,
The swift and silent lizard of the stones!

"Not all," the echoes answer me,—"not all!
Prophetic sounds and loud arise forever
From us and from all ruin unto the wise,

As melody from Memnon to the sun.
We rule the hearts of mightiest men, we rule
With a despotic sway all giant minds.
We are not impotent,—we pallid stones.
Not all our power is gone, not all our fame,
Not all the magic of our high renown,
Not all the wonder that encircles us,
Not all the mysteries that in us lie,
Not all the memories that hang upon
And cling around about us as a garment,
Clothing us in a robe of more than glory."

Edgar Allan Poe, *The Colosseum*, 1835

It is no fiction, but plain, sober, honest Truth, to say: so suggestive and distinct is it at this hour: that, for a moment—actually in passing in—they who will, may have the whole great pile before them, as it used to be, with thousands of eager faces staring down into the arena, and such a whirl of strife, and blood, and dust going on there, as no language can describe. Its solitude, its awful beauty, and its utter desolation, strike upon the stranger the next moment, like a softened sorrow; and never in his life, perhaps, will he be so moved and overcome by any sight, not immediately connected with his own affections and afflictions.

To see it crumbling there, an inch a year; its walls and arches overgrown with green; its corridors open to the day; the long grass growing in its porches; young trees of yesterday, springing up on its ragged parapets, and bearing fruit: chance produce of the seeds dropped there by the birds who build their nests within its chinks and crannies; to see its Pit of Fight filled up with earth, and the peaceful Cross planted in the centre; to climb into its upper halls, and look down on ruin, ruin, ruin, all about it; the triumphal arches of Constantine, Septimus Severus, and Titus; the Roman Forum; the Palace of the Cæsars; the temples of the old religion, fallen down and gone; is to see the ghost of old Rome, wicked, wonderful old city, haunting the very ground on which its people trod. It is the most impressive, the most stately, the most solemn, grand, majestic, mournful sight, conceivable. Never, in its bloodiest prime, can the sight of the gigantic Coliseum, full and running over with the lustiest life, have moved one's heart, as it must move all who look upon it now, a ruin. God be thanked: a ruin!

Charles Dickens, *Pictures from Italy*, 1846

By Moonlight, Posing for the Grand Tour

Rudolph Ritter von Alt, *The Colosseum*,
1835, watercolour on paper, Hamburg,
Kunsthalle

The object of the present little volume is to call the attention of the lover of the works of creation to those floral productions which flourish, in triumph, upon the ruins of a single building. Flowers are perhaps the most graceful and most lovely objects of the creation but are not at any time, more delightful than when associated with what recalls to the memory time and place, and especially that of generations long passed away. They form a link m the memory, and teach us hopeful and soothing lessons, amid the sadness of bygone ages: and cold indeed must be the heart that does not respond to their silent appeal; for, though without speech, they tell of that regenerating power which reanimates the dust of mouldering greatness, and clothes their sad and fallen grandeur with graceful forms and curiously constructed leaves and flowers, resplendent with their gay and various colours, and perfume the air with their exquisite odours.

The plants which we have found growing upon the Colosseum, and have here described, amount to no less a number than 420 species; in this number there are examples of 258 Genera, and illustrations of 66 of the Natural Orders of plants, a number which seems almost incredible. There are 56 species of grass – 47 of the order *compositae* or syngenetic plants — and 41 of the Leguminous or Pea tribe: but it must be remembered that, though the ground occupied by the building is about six acres, the surface of the walls and lodgement on the ruins upon which they grow is much more extensive, and the variety of soil is much greater than would be supposed without examination; for, on the lower north side, it is damp, and favourable to the production of many plants, while the upper walls and accumulated mould are warmer and dryer, and, consequently, better suited for the development of others: and, on the south side, it is hot and dry, and suited only for the growth of differently constructed tribes.

The collection of the plants and the species noted has been made some years; but, since that time, many of the plants have been destroyed, from the alterations and restorations that have been made in the ruins; a circumstance that cannot but be lamented. To preserve a further falling of any portion is most desirable; but to carry the restorations, and the brushing and cleaning, to the extent to which it has been subjected, instead of leaving it in its wild and solemn grandeur, is to destroy the impression and solitary lesson which so magnificent a ruin is calculated to make upon the mind...

This extremely beautiful early spring flower [the anemone], is very generally distributed in shady places in all parts of the South of Europe; it varies in colour, from a pale pink, to a deep rose colour, according to the more or less exposed situation in which it grows. It is one of the species of anemone commonly cultivated as a border-flower. It grows in various parts of the Colosseum, and there flowers freely, glowing in its bright colours like a joyous star upon the mouldering remains of past generations...

Richard Deakin, *Flora of the Colosseum of Rome*, 1855

By Moonlight, Posing for the Grand Tour

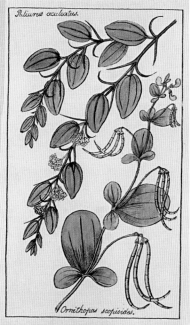

Richard Deakin, illustrations by *Flora of the Colosseum of Rome, or Illustrations and Descriptions of Four Hundred and Twenty Plants Growing Spontaneously upon the Ruins of the Colosseum of Rome*, 1855, London, Groombridge, 1873

Abraham-Louis-Rodolphe Ducros,
Interior of the Colosseum, 1787-1793,
pencil, watercolour and gouache with
strokes of pen, ink and paint on two
sheets of paper applied to canvas,
72.6 x 101.6 cm, Stourhead, The Hoare
Collection

Inside the monument Ducros depicts a small group
of elegant visitors: the ladies are distributing alms to
a family of beggars, while their companion admires
the grandiosity of the architecture; in the
background a crowd of pilgrims participates in a
religious ceremony.

As usual of a moonlight evening, several carriages stood at the entrance of this famous ruin, and the precincts and interior were anything but a solitude. The French sentinel on duty beneath the principal archway eyed our party curiously, but offered no obstacle to their admission. Within, the moonlight filled and flooded the great empty space; it glowed upon tier above tier of ruined, grass-grown arches, and made them even too distinctly visible. The splendor of the revelation took away that inestimable effect of dimness and mystery by which the imagination might be assisted to build a grander structure than the Coliseum, and to shatter it with a more picturesque decay. Byron's celebrated description is better than the reality. He beheld the scene in his mind's eye, through the witchery of many intervening years, and faintly illuminated it as if with starlight instead of this broad glow of moonshine.

The party of our friends sat down, three or four of them on a prostrate column, another on a shapeless lump of marble, once a Roman altar; others on the steps of one of the Christian shrines [...] There was much pastime and gayety just then in the area of the Coliseum [...]. Some youths and maidens were running merry races across the open space, and playing at hide and seek a little way within the duskiness of the ground tier of arches, whence now and then you could hear the half-shriek, half laugh of a frolicsome girl, whom the shadow had betrayed into a young man's arms. Elder groups were seated on the fragments of pillars and blocks of marble that lay round the verge of the arena, talking in the quick, short ripple of the Italian tongue. On the steps of the great black cross in the centre of the Coliseum sat a party singing scraps of songs, with much laughter and merriment between the stanzas.

It was a strange place for song and mirth. That black cross marks one of the special blood-spots of the earth [...]. From all this crime and suffering, however, the spot has derived a more than common sanctity. An inscription promises seven years' indulgence, seven years of remission from the pains of purgatory, and earlier enjoyment of heavenly bliss, for each separate kiss imprinted on the black cross. [...] Besides its central consecration, the whole area has been made sacred by a range of shrines [...]. In accordance with an ordinary custom, a pilgrim was making his progress from shrine to shrine upon his knees, and saying a penitential prayer at each. Light-footed girls ran across the path along which he crept, or sported with their friends close by the shrines where he was kneeling. The pilgrim took no heed, and the girls meant no irreverence; for in Italy religion jostles along side by side with business and sport, after a fashion of its own, and people are accustomed to kneel down and pray, or see others praying, between two fits of merriment, or between two sins.

To make an end of our description, a red twinkle of light was visible amid the breadth of shadow that fell across the upper part of the Coliseum. Now it glimmered through a line of arches, or threw a broader gleam as it rose out of some profound abyss of ruin; now it was muffled by a heap of shrubbery which had adventurously clambered to that dizzy height; and so the red light kept ascending to loftier and loftier ranges of the structure, until it stood like a star where the blue sky rested against the Coliseum's topmost wall. It indicated a party of English or Americans paying the inevitable visit by moonlight, and exalting themselves with raptures that were Byron's, not their own.

Nathaniel Hawthorne, *The Marble Faun*, 1860

Ippolito Caffi, *Fireworks inside the Colosseum*, c.1845, oil on paper applied to canvas, 25.5 x 41.5 cm, Rome, Museo di Roma

The relative solitude of a romantic walk was abruptly interrupted when the Colosseum was transformed into the site of firework displays for the enjoyment of a cheering and enthusiastic crowd. The false fire inside the Colosseum which animated the red glow of the walls, arches and columns, represented a particular exciting vision for those crowded close to the building. In order to depict the scene, Caffi chose a close-up view, and accentuated the dramatic nature of the image by contrasting the blackness of the shadows, the red glow of the blazing surfaces, the blinding white lights at the heart of the scene and the greens reflected under the vaults of the arches. Evidently, in addition to his interest in the theatrical effects of the nocturnal festival, Caffi the artist and patriot, desired to get across a clear political meaning (Federica Pirani).

By Moonlight, Posing for the Grand Tour

MICHAEL ANGELO. Behold,
How wonderful it is ! The queen of flowers,
The marble rose of Rome ! Its petals torn
By wind and rain of thrice five hundred years;
Its mossy sheath half rent away, and sold
To ornament our palaces and churches,
Or to be trodden under feet of man
Upon the Tiber s bank; yet what remains
Still opening its fair bosom to the sun,
And to the constellations that at night
Hang poised above it like a swarm of bees.

CAVALIERI. The rose of Rome, but not of Paradise;
Not the white rose our Tuscan poet saw,
With saints for petals. When this rose was perfect
Its hundred thousand petals were not saints,
But senators in their Thessalian caps,
And all the roaring populace of Rome;
And even an Empress and the Vestal Virgins,
Who came to see the gladiators die,
Could not give sweetness to a rose like this.

MICHAEL ANGELO. I spake not of its uses, but its beauty.

CAVALIERI. The sand beneath our feet is saturate
With blood of martyrs; and these rifted stones
Are awful witnesses against a people
Whose pleasure was the pain of dying men.

MICHAEL ANGELO. Tomaso Cavalieri, on my word,
You should have been a preacher, not a painter !
Think you that I approve such cruelties,
Because I marvel at the architects
Who built these walls, and curved these noble arches ?
Oh, I am put to shame, when I consider
How mean our work is, when compared with theirs !
Look at these walls about us and above us !
They have been shaken by earthquakes, have been made

A fortress, and been battered by long sieges;
The iron clamps, that held the stones together,
Have been wrenched from them; but they stand erect
And firm, as if they had been hewn and hollowed
Out of the solid rock, and were a part
Of the foundations of the world itself.

CAVALIERI. Your work, I say again, is nobler work,
In so far as its end and aim are nobler;
And this is but a ruin, like the rest.
Its vaulted passages are made the caverns
Of robbers, and are haunted by the ghosts
Of murdered men.

MICHAEL ANGELO. A thousand wild flowers bloom
From every chink, and the birds build their nests
Among the ruined arches, and suggest
New thoughts of beauty to the architect.
Now let us climb the broken stairs that lead
Into the corridors above, and study
The marvel and the mystery of that art
In which I am a pupil, not a master.
All things must have an end; the world itself
Must have an end, as in a dream I saw it.
There came a great hand out of heaven, and touched
The earth, and stopped it in its course. The seas
Leaped, a vast cataract, into the abyss…

Henry Wadsworth Longfellow, *Michael Angelo*, 1869

By Moonlight, Posing for the Grand Tour

Joseph Mallord William Turner, *The Colosseum, Rome, by Moonlight*, 1819, watercolour, tempera and pencil on paper, 23.2 x 36.9 cm, London, Tate

Gustave Moreau, *Rome, View of the Colosseum*, 1858, watercolour, 22.5 x 28.5 cm, Paris, Musée Gustave Moreau

Rome, 18th June 1871 – Rome has become a whitewashed sepulchre. The houses, and even the ancient and revered palaces, are coated with white; the rust of centuries is scraped away, and we now see, for the first time, how architecturally ugly Rome really is. Rosa has shaved even the Colosseum — that is to say, has cleared away all the plants that made it so beautiful. The Flora of the Colosseum, on which Deakin, an Englishman, wrote a book some years ago, has thus been destroyed. This transformation of the sacred city into a secular, is the reverse of the time when, with a like enthusiasm, pagan Rome transformed herself into a spiritual city.

Gregorovius, *The Roman Journals*, 1852-1874

By Moonlight, Posing for the Grand Tour

Maurice Denis, *The Colosseum*, c.1898, oil on
paper, 20.5 x 33.5 cm, private collection

There was a waning moon in the sky, and her radiance was not brilliant, but she was veiled in a thin cloud-curtain which seemed to diffuse and equalize it. When, on his return from the villa (it was eleven o'clock), Winterbourne approached the dusky circle of the Colosseum, it recurred to him, as a lover of the picturesque, that the interior, in the pale moonshine, would be well worth a glance. He turned aside and walked to one of the empty arches, near which, as he observed, an open carriage—one of the little Roman street-cabs—was stationed. Then he passed in, among the cavernous shadows of the great structure, and emerged upon the clear and silent arena. The place had never seemed to him more impressive. One-half of the gigantic circus was in deep shade, the other was sleeping in the luminous dusk. As he stood there he began to murmur Byron's famous lines, out of "Manfred;" but before he had finished his quotation he remembered that if nocturnal meditations in the Colosseum are recommended by the poets, they are deprecated by the doctors. The historic atmosphere was there, certainly; but the historic atmosphere, scientifically considered, was no better than a villainous miasma. Winterbourne walked to the middle of the arena, to take a more

By Moonlight, Posing for the Grand Tour

general glance, intending thereafter to make a hasty retreat. The great cross in the centre was covered with shadow; it was only as he drew near it that he made it out distinctly. Then he saw that two persons were stationed upon the low steps which formed its base. One of these was a woman, seated; her companion was standing in front of her. Presently the sound of the woman's voice came to him distinctly in the warm night air. "Well, he looks at us as one of the old lions or tigers may have looked at the Christian martyrs!" These were the words he heard, in the familiar accent of Miss Daisy Miller.

"Let us hope he is not very hungry," responded the ingenious Giovanelli. "He will have to take me first; you will serve for dessert!"

Henry James, *Daisy Miller*, 1878

David Roberts, *Interior of the Colosseum at Sunset with Figures*, 1850s, oil on canvas, 28.5 x 87 cm, Rome, Galleria W. Apolloni Collection

Then I went to the Colosseum. The enormous mass, the collapsed side with its openings silhouetted in blue. Vaulted corridors open everywhere, their eaten steps are like slides. The colossus is like a stone lace, with blue holes. Above is a light blue sky, very clear and dappled with small clouds flying. How could one pull the awning over? The evocation of this immense circus, packed with crowds, with her eight thousand (?) spectators, the Emperor's balcony and, underneath, the Vestals. A ruin cooked by the sun, golden, majestic and still gigantic despite her half collapsed state.

Émile Zola, *Travel Diary*, 1894

By Moonlight, Posing for the Grand Tour

Christoffer Wilhelm Eckersberg, *A View through Three of the North-Western Arches of the Third Storey of the Coliseum*, 1815 or 1816, oil on canvas, 32 x 49.5 cm, Copenhagen, Statens Museum for Kunst

In this painting, one of the masterpieces from his stay in Rome, the Danish painter seems to want to experiment and anticipate *en plein air* painting.

But the horizon expanded towards the southeast, and beyond the arches of Titus and Constantine he perceived the Colosseum. Ah! that colossus, only one-half or so of which has been destroyed by time as with the stroke of a mighty scythe, it rises in its enormity and majesty like a stone lace-work with hundreds of empty bays agape against the blue of heaven! There is a world of halls, stairs, landings, and passages, a world where one loses oneself amidst death-like silence and solitude.

The furrowed tiers of seats, eaten into by the atmosphere, are like shapeless steps leading down into some old extinct crater, some natural circus excavated by the force of the elements in indestructible rock. The hot suns of eighteen hundred years have baked and scorched this ruin, which has reverted to a state of nature, bare and golden-brown like a mountain-side, since it has been stripped of its vegetation, the flora which once made it like a virgin forest. And what an evocation when the mind sets flesh and blood and life again on all that!

Émile Zola, *Roma*, 1896

Jean-Baptiste Camille Corot, *The Coliseum
seen through the Arches of the Basilica of
Constantine*, 1825, oil on paper applied to
canvas, 23 x 35 cm, Paris, Musée du Louvre

In Italy, through foreign painters who go there for the
Grand Tour, the landscape itself, and not the idea of
nature, would eventually become the subject of the
work, freeing itself from picturesque anecdotes. This
study from life demonstrates this, more free in its
method and spontaneous in atmospheric merits which,
despite the classical rationality of the composition,
captures clear volumes by combining flat brushstrokes
with tonal values which the colours assume, considering
the intensity of the light in the wake of the teaching of
Thomas Jones.

The Symbol of an Empire

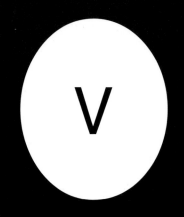

"It is not without reason that of all the places laden with glory that Rome boasts as her incredible privilege before the world, I have chosen the Colosseum, this immense monument, this everlasting testimony of Rome". It was in these terms that Mussolini would appeal to the *avanguardisti* of the Fascist Youth gathered at the Colosseum on the 28th October 1926, on the fourth anniversary of the glorious March on Rome. In the booklet published the following year by the *Opera Nazionale Balilla* one finds, pasted on the orange cover, a photo of an event which shows an arena filled to capacity, an animated view of the gatherings which will be replicated many times, in a carefully prepared theatre of rhetoric in black images and chromolithographs which appeared on the illustrated magazines of the era. The majesty of the amphitheatre imposes itself on the background of moments to be immortalised – such as the unusual greeting of the Duce, who in 1926 met Gabriele d'Annunzio upon a camel, in a moment immortalised by a rare postcard – or for use in sinister photomontages for a propagandist use of the most powerful symbol of an expanding empire, which Fascism systematically appropriated along with others in the construction of a great new Rome. The era of "pickaxe renovation" had indeed begun, the tool-icon of frantic activism to isolate, laboriously, in order to emphasise the principal monuments of antiquity, esteemed as an arsenal of myths, a deposit of progressive destinies but perhaps also – as some have supposed – a target of resentment which Mussolini harboured since youth against the Eternal City. The urban landscape of the Capital was shedding its skin at many points, as is revealed by bombastic aeropainting, and the proud Via dell'Impero which at last bound the Colosseum to the heart of Rome, with an unparalleled perspective, ideal for thundering military parades and triumphal pomp. Memorable yet grim was the staging of the arrival of Hitler in May 1938. Intoxicated by the Greek beauty of the *Discobulus* which he desired to bring back with him, embodying the ideal Olympic ethics which Leni Riefenstahl was evoking in her aestheticising films, the Führer along with his architects had sought to recreate in Nuremberg, the sacred city of Nazism, an area for rallies which would artificially equal those of Rome: even today, between fascination and fear, one can look over the vast terraces of the Kongreßhalle, which in its forms attempted to mimic the model of the Flavian Amphitheatre, influencing the masses. Mussolini also tried his hand at a similar operation by assigning a prominent role to the Palazzo della Civiltà Italiana, more famously known as the "Square Colosseum", within the site of EUR: that glacial, metaphysical petrifaction able to embody and transmit the values of fascist civilisation, moulding the character of the generations into a national identity of a people of warriors and builders. The ambitious project was alas begun when the regime was heading towards meltdown. In the June of '44, American armoured vehicles would parade by the Colosseum among exultant crowds.

The Symbol of an Empire

The flags of Fascist Italy and Nazi Germany
wave before the Colosseum, on occasion of
the visit of the Führer to Italy, 3 – 9 May
1938, from the album *The journey of the
Führer in Italy*

The speech of Benito Mussolini to the
Fascist Youth at the Colosseum, Rome,
28th October 1926, Year V, by the Opera
Nazionale Balilla, Carrara, Istituto
Editoriale Fascista Apuano, 1927

The Symbol of an Empire

On the fourth anniversary of the March on Rome, the Hon. Mussolini spoke to the *avantguardisti* of the Capital and Central Italy, gathered at the Colosseum, who gave vibrant support to the Duce of Fascism. Drawing by Alfredo Ortelli for "Illustrazione del Popolo", 7th November 1926

AN INSCRIPTION IN PIECES. "In the twenty sixth year of the reign of King Victor Emmanuel III, in the fourth year since the restoration and renovation of Italy at the hands of the Duce Benito Mussolini": thus recited the inscription reduced to fragments after the fall of Fascism, like many other containing the name of the Duce which adorned public monuments condemned to *damnatio memoriae*. To this we should add that Mussolini, as part of the measures promoted by the Fascist regime within the Colosseum, trusting on a return to the operation, had healed the ancient *vulnus* left by the removal of the Cross (erected, as we have seen, by Benedict XIV in the centre of the arena in 1750, when he consecrated the monument to the Martyrs) and the excavations of the hypogea between 1874 and 1875. He had in fact sought to place a new cross on the northern side where we can still admire it, perhaps to dampen the possible anxieties of the Church, juxtaposing on its base a political inscription alongside a religious one which remembered the merit of the pontificate of Pius XI.

Speech by Victor Emmanuel III at the Colosseum
to the gathering of the *Alpini* in 1926

La grande adunata nel Colosseo. Il Duce parla a diecimila operai milanesi convenuti alla Capitale per riaffermare la loro fedeltà al Regime. (Disegno di A. Beltrame).

The large gathering at the Colosseum.
The Duce speaks to ten thousand Milanese
workers who gathered in the Capital to reaffirm
their loyalty to the regime, drawing by
A. Beltrame for "La Domenica del Corriere",
13th May 1928. This was the first occasion
in which the magazine used the word "Duce"

The Symbol of an Empire

Workers clean the Colosseum, perhaps after
a gathering, 1930s

Tato (Guglielmo Sansoni), *Flying over the Colosseum in a Spiral (Spiraling)*, 1930, oil on canvas, 80 x 80 cm, Rome, Ventura Collection

The painting, constituting one of the most effective expressions of futurist aeropainting, which after the media coverage of D'Annunzio's flights (fruit of the theories of Giulio Douhet), found favour in the regime due to their euphoric and aggressive air technological dominance which dovetailed with the creation of the Italian *Regia Aeronautica* by Mussolini. A preview was perhaps given by the archaeological surveys from above which were carried out by Giacomo Boni in collaboration with military engineers on the Via Sacra at the turn of the century, while at the same time Filippo Masoero produced dynamic views from aerial photography between 1927 and 1937: the one of the Comitium likely dates from 1934.

This time is the Piazza del Colosseo which generates the centrifugal motion of the aircraft, which transforms and synthesises in its movement the details of a city in light, colour and speed, according to the rules of the *Futurist Manifesto of Aeropainting*, written in 1929 by Filippo Tommaso Marinetti and other artists, including Tato. Also in this case the main focus is the amphitheatre, more schematically included in the celebrated *Aeroportrait of Benito Mussolini the Aviator*, also from 1930. Here Imperial glory shines from the proud face of the Duce who, like an inspired genius of solar luminosity, is creating a Third Rome.

The Symbol of an Empire

Alfredo Gauro Ambrosi, *Aeroportrait
of Benito Mussolini the Aviator*, 1930,
oil on canvas, 124 x 124 cm, Rome,
private collection

IL MATTINO ILLUSTRATO

Anno IX - N. 46 - 14 - 21 Novembre 1932 (Anno XI)
SI PUBBLICA OGNI SETTIMANA — PREZZO CENT. 40

ROMA, 28 OTTOBRE DELL'ANNO UNDECIMO: IL DUCE, a cavallo, alla testa di tredici legioni di mutilati inaugura la nuova Via dell'Impero, muovendo dal Colosseo verso l'Altare della Patria (fot. Luce riprodotta a colori)

Rome, 28th October of the eleventh year:
the Duce, on horseback, at the head of
thirteen legions of wounded veterans,
inaugurates the new Via dell'Impero,
moving from the Colosseum towards the
Altar of the Fatherland, Luce photograph
reproduced in colour for the cover of "Il
Mattino Illustrato", 14 – 21 November 1932

The Symbol of an Empire

Ceremonies of the VIII Fascist Levy on Via dell'Impero. Mussolini, De Bono and other authorities on horseback inspect the Fascist Youth arrayed around the Colosseum in 1934

The parade of the youth of the Opera
Nazionale Balilla along Via dell'Impero,
3rd April 1936

With the ravages and demolitions of the Fascist Era,
the impressions of Rome which had so struck the
travellers of the nineteenth century disappear: "Little by
little from the narrow alleys Ancient Rome begins to
emerge, and at last there, where the living city ends,
growing larger between secular ivy, aloe and open
plains, with the vast Colosseum, triumphal arches and
ruins of the Palaces of the Caesars (N. Gogol, *Roma*
[1824], Rome 1945). The judgement that emerges from
one of the articles published in the "Giornale d'Italia" is
rather different however, on the occasion of the final
works before the opening of Via dell'Impero: "the old
giant has shaken off the ancient solitude and has taken
to becoming a pivot for the circular motion of cars,
which all but touch the venerable stones of the Via
Sacra with their tyres."

The Symbol of an Empire

Blessing of the vehicles arrayed around the
Colosseum during the Feast of Santa
Francesca Romana, patron saint of
motorists, 9th March 1935

Bruno Munari, Cover of "La Rivista
illustrata del Popolo d'Italia", a. XIV, no. 4,
April 1936

The illustration is dedicated to the Birth of Rome
which falls on the 21st April, the day on which the
Fascist Era was celebrated along with Labour Day.
Hence the view, simple yet symbolically effective,
between the grey travertine shape of the Colosseum on
a horizon of a blue sky dotted with clouds, and the high
chimney in brick, cut in the foreground, from which a
small fasces and a waving tricolor: it could take the
same ideological meaning of the obelisks erected in
Imperial and Baroque Rome, yet this time in honour of
the workers of modern Italy.

Alberto Salietti, Cover of "La Rivista
illustrata del Popolo d'Italia", a. XV, no. 5-6,
May-June 1937

The allusion to the power of the Fascist Empire is also
clear in this drawing – in which the Colosseum serves
as impressive scenery – with reference to the recent
victory in Ethiopia, evoked by the parade of soldiers
through the triumphal arch and by the display of
archaeological calligraphy, trophies of war and the
ethnic Obelisk of Axum, recently returned by the
Italian State.

The Symbol of an Empire

LA DOMENICA DEL CORRIERE

ITALIA	ESTERO		
Anno . . . . L. 19,—	L. 40,—	Si pubblica a Milano ogni settimana	Uffici del giornale: Via Solferino, 28 - Milano
Semestre . . . . . . » 10,—	» 21,—	Supplemento illustrato del "Corriere della Sera"	Per tutti gli articoli e illustrazioni è riservata la proprietà letteraria e artistica, secondo le leggi e i trattati internazionali.

Anno 40 — N. 20   15 Maggio 1938 - XVI   Centesimi 40 la copia

Il trionfale arrivo di Hitler a Roma.
La berlina col Re Imperatore e il Führer, lungo la via dell'Impero fantasticamente illuminata.
(Disegno di A. Beltrame)

The triumphant arrival of Hitler in Rome. The
sedan with the King Emperor and the Führer
along a fantastically illuminated Via dell'Impero.
Drawing by A. Beltrame for "La Domenica del
Corriere", 15th May 1938

181

Portrait of Mussolini with Hitler during the
visit of the Führer to Italy; in the
background we see the crowd and the
Colosseum. "Il Mattino illustrato",
9 – 16 May 1938

Two views of the Kongreßhalle of Nuremberg, a form of modern Colosseum conceived for Hitler by Ludwig and Franz Ruff, left unfinished due to the outbreak of World War II

A scale model inside the Documentation Centre of the rally area of the National Socialist Party shows the grandiose original project. Hitler was intoxicated by the magnificence of the amphitheatre so much that he took it as a model, since he had time to observe the architectural design, having to shelter inside it due to rain which had somewhat reduced the program of military parades.

American tanks parade alongside the
Colosseum after the liberation of Rome,
5th June 1944

The Symbol of an Empire

Roman citizens rejoice at the Colosseum
for the liberation

A surreal and metacartographic image which unites
the glory of Ancient and Future Rome with the their
epicentres, which allude to the elliptical Colosseum
and the so called "Square Colosseum". The warm
tones of the old village, greatly beloved by members
of the Roman School, clash with the rationalist and
immobile "white city", destined to remain a long
lasting vision due to the fact that work on its
construction was interrupted by the global conflict, a
ghost of that "ideal city" which for many years was
made of enigmatic buildings shrouded in nothing, a
magical theatre which would have bewitched the
masters of Cinema, such as Fellini, in the dream of
timeless architecture.

The Symbol of an Empire

Giorgio Quaroni, *Allegory of Fame*, 1939,
watercolour and tempera on paper, 54.5 x
43.5 cm, Rome, private collection

Break hour on the site of the 1942 World Fair of Rome, in front of the Palazzo della Civiltà Italiana, 1940

Without a doubt the the most inspired building of modernised "Romanism" and the "Spiritual heart" of E42, the "Square Colosseum" is called to immediately and fully visualise the link between the Flavian Amphitheatre, used at least as the imaginative base – and a beautiful 1930 canvas with the Colosseum of Achille Funi, decorator of the Palazzo dei Congressi, today conserved at the Galleria Comunale d'Arte Moderna e Contemporanea in Rome – reworked in the intelligent and refined, yet synthetic and schematic language of rationalism, in a volumetric but not dimensional space. The arch as a Roman architectural emblem is the model repeated in the six orders of the four identical façades, but also the series of large allegorical statues planned for the loggias, recall the Colosseum as the crowning attic created in order to add on each side the inscription with the famous phrase of the Duce: "A People of Poets, of Artists, of Heroes, of Saints, of Thinkers, of Scientists, of Navigators and Travellers". The external travertine façade acts as a clever concealment of the "modern" reinforced concrete skeleton, with an interplay of chiaroscuro between inside and outside, between blinding light and deep shadow, accentuated in artificial light, as well as the golden and classical shell of the amphitheatre hid the most futuristic technological and constructive solutions of the interior. The heavy reworking undertaken by Marcello Piacentini to the rigorous and winning plan of the Gruppo Guerrini-La Padula-Romano, of a an overcoming lightness, had in fact conferred on the Palazzo an monumentality alien to the designers, who came to reject the authorship of the building, at the heart of a recent work of high esteem.

The Symbol of an Empire

A Ring-a-Ring o' Roses in EUR.
In the background stands the completed
Palazzo della Civiltà Italiana

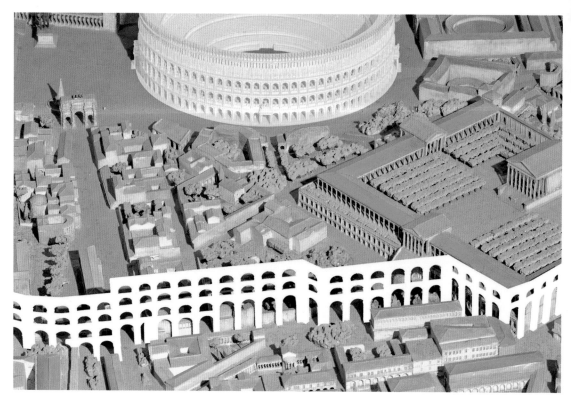

Olivo Barbieri, *site specific_ROMA 04 14*

The alienating images of the Emilian photographer
reveal a mode of selective vision, slow and at the
same time dynamic, for this reason between the true
Rome and the scale city of the huge maquette
displayed in the Museo della Civiltà Romana in
EUR, between Ancient and Fascist Rome there
seems to be no difference, especially when the idea of
the Colosseum is artificially compared to its
representation. This is even more evident from the
slow distortion from above towards the Square
Colosseum, erected like a temple on a stylobate and
slotted into the orthogonal cage of spaces, no longer
physically empty but instead psychological, in
comparison with the incongruous accumulation of
history which underlines the cold mass of an
amphitheatre and an aqueduct, with their hypnotic
sequence of arches.

The Symbol of an Empire

Olivo Barbieri, *site specific_ROMA 04 14*

A Myth of Our Time

Behind us lies a splendid civilisation, made of human ightness; we have the Apollo of Veii, we have the classical spirits, the great Greek beauty. But one has to destroy it voluntarily, so that not so much as a memory remains of it. One needs to bring down the Colosseum and remake it similarly out in plastic. We must live and understand only this ocean o silent objects which surround it". We read of this neo-futurist testimony in an interview, indeed titled *The Plastic Colosseum*, conducted by Andrea Barbato for "L'Espresso" on the 11th April 1965, which was recently rediscovered by Andrea Cortellessa. The speaker is Goffredo Parise, remembering that long journey in the United States which had been decisive for the discovery of the fantasy and extravagance of the true "modern" art of those wonderful years, in which he began to follow "Pop of Piazza del Popolo, whose young meetings were held at the Gran Teatro which was then the Galleria della Tartaruga, with the somewhat despotic director, Plinio de Martiis". While both the intense black and white images of Herbert List, and an entire photographic service in colour by Robert Capa published in the magazine "Holiday" in April 1952 and other shots by the author encouraged the spread abroad in the '50's, together with cinema, of the image of *Eternal Rome* through her piazzas and monuments, pop art on the other hand considered the Colosseum, the Wolf, the frescoes of the Sistine Chapel as symbols of Italian culture, comparing them to the 210 bottles of Coca-Cola or the cans of Campbell's Soup with the label ripped off, which perfectly represented American identity. Tano Festa understood this: "An American paints Coca-Cola, for me Michelangelo is the same thing, in the sense that we are in a country where instead of consuming food in a box, we consume the Mona Lisa on chocolates". He continues: "I am sorry for the Americans who have so little history on their shoulders, but for an Italian artist, a Roman who mostly lived a stone's throw from the Vatican walls, the Sistine Chapel is *popular*". With this awareness Renato Mambor operates on his enamel coated canvases, in which the unmistakable outline of the Colosseum is graphical y treated on neutral planes, together with zebras and colourful butterflies juxtaposed in bizarre scale ratios. Pino Pascali assembles wooden panels to form a curve of the amphitheatre and attaches it to a wall after having covered it with a canvas, in order to paint on top of that row of arches, so large as to permit one to lay underneath as if one was pretending to be at *Italia in miniatura*, which was to be born some years later. The reflection on such a particular form of monument also inspired Luca Maria Patella, who artificially recreated it by photographing the Colosseum with a wide angle effect in the wake of a car – in the foreground we see the enlarged arrow marking on the road to indicate the direction   and with a scarf resting on the ground to close the ellipse, in a dynamic and futurist shot which also influenced the 1988 *Nighttime Navigator* and the canvases which were computerised with the Colosseum, which Mario Schifano would create in the last decade of the 20th century. In Italian pop art the past, having become landscape and art, beats a modern life which is always filtered through a historic condition, whose symbols and myths are not skyscrapers but the Colosseum and the Roman Fora (Achille Bonito Oliva).

A Myth of Our Time

Herbert List, *Rome, Trattoria at the
Colosseo*, 1951

A Myth of Our Time

Even an American artist from *Action Painting*, while travelling in Rome, was struck by the Colosseum which he portrayed twice, from the outside and inside. In the dizzying bottleneck of steps and overhangs of the arena, the painter seems to materially echo the Dantesque Circles from the illustrations of the *Divine Comedy*, while the profile of the city just emerges, by means of synthetic strokes of a spatula, from the wide chasm, a geological and historical emblem of an urban destiny.

William Grosvenor Congdon, *Rome – Colosseum 2*, 1951, oil and enamel on masonite, 99 x 127 cm, Milano, The William G. Congdon Foundation

A Myth of Our Time

Luca Maria Patella, *Scarf and Colosseum*,
1966, cibachrome, 100 x 100 cm, Rome,
Dello Schiavo Collection

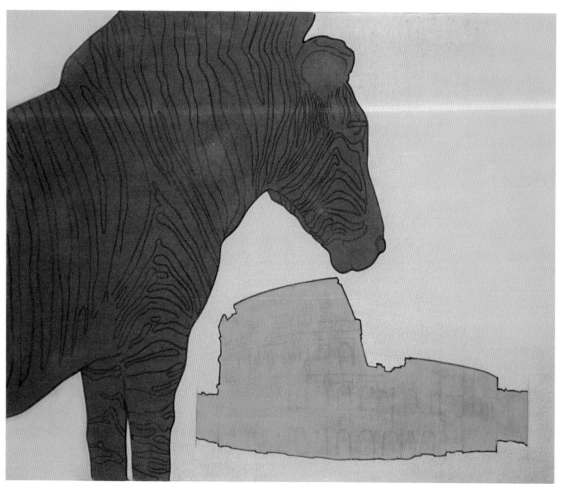

Renato Mambor, *Zebra and Colosseum*,
1965, industrial enamel on raw canvas,
118 x 142 cm, Rome, Dello Schiavo Collection

A Myth of Our Time

Renato Mambor, *Colosseum and Butterfly*,
1966, enamel and acrylic on canvas,
70 x 100 cm, Patrizia and Blu Mambor collection

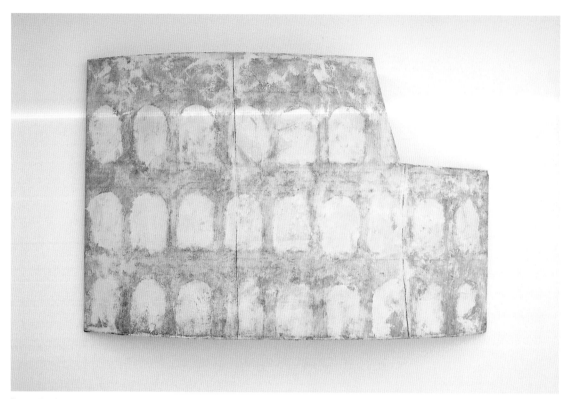

Pino Pascali, *Colosseum*, 1964, tempera on cloth
and canvas on wood, 166 x 260 x 33 cm,
Reggio Emilia, Maramotti Collection

Plinio De Martiis, *Pino Pascali and his "Colosseum"
at the "Tortoise" Gallery"*, 1965, gelatin print,
59 x 49 cm, Latina, Archivio di Stato

Superstudio – a Florentine group of the most influential radical architects – has since 1969 published photomontages of the Continuous Monument in specialist magazines, denouncing in metaphysically dry images the impossibility of any operation in the city and its territory according to traditional criteria, and demonstrates to young generations of architects and designers the opportunity to instead generate poetic and autobiographical forms, produced by a critical contamination of diverse cultures.

In Rome, the Continuous Monument became a superelevation of the Colosseum: its structural grid replicates the rhythm of the latter's pilaster strips and entablature, and its rationalist openings dovetail with the original archways.

There is perhaps no building in the world which has played so iconic a role, whilst at the same time expressing functional requests at the highest level. In Rome this also happens in a negative way, for example in the kilometer of Corviale. As stated by Superstudio, "architecture is to time what salt is to water". Once its symbolic image has melted, architecture reveals its true purpose, to be inhabited. But to do this you need a new plan. Thus the process is circular.

A Myth of Our Time

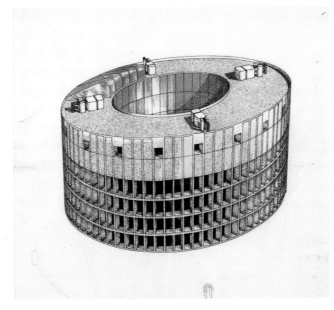

Superstudio, *The Continuous Monument. Grand Hotel Colosseum*, second version, 1969, india ink, halftone screen b/n, pencil on tracing paper, Rome, MAXXI National Museum of 21st century Arts, MAXXI Architecture Collection, Fondo Superstudio

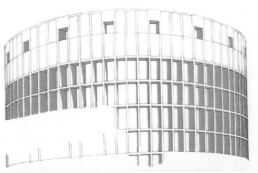

Superstudio, *The Continuous Monument. Grand Hotel Colosseum*, 1969, china, halftone screen and pencil on tracing paper, Rome, MAXXI National Museum of 21st century Arts, MAXXI Architecture Collection, Fondo Superstudio

Superstudio, *The Continuous Monument. Grand Hotel Colosseum*, first version, 1969, india ink, heliotype on cardboard, Rome, MAXXI, MAXXI National Museum of 21st century Arts, MAXXI Architecture Collection, Fondo Superstudio

The numerous paintings of Renato Guttuso, all from 1972, face the "half brazier, half ossuary" Colosseum from many angles. Guttuso gives us a ruin which has been dramatically stripped, covered in ashes which look like snow and a colourful glimpse of Mediterranean history on a starry night. Here it appears, isolated as in a still life in the *Funerali di Togliatti* to unequivocally indicate the place of a crowded funeral dominated by a fiery Roman sunset, in which the painter himself participates, with clenched fist upon a scaffold, so involved and absorbed in this pictorial enterprise to write it in the news.

This would become the Manifesto of the Italian Communist Party which Guttuso insisted to the Direction that he finish in Bologna, the city then considered the best example of good governance from the Left: a large secular liturgy who gives its last respects to a charismatic leader with whom the artist had publicly clashed so many years before. To Togliatti who in 1948 had attacked painters, mostly communists, for having put together an exhibition of "monstrous things, horrors and nonsense" and lacking the content that a class struggle required, Guttuso responded in kind by defending the freedom of art, which could be useful only if it was true expression and non merely naturalistic illustration. He had after all already written in 1941 in an edition of "Primato": It is not necessary for a painter to be of of party or another, or to make war o revolution, but it necessary that acts, in painting, as one who acts in war or revolution. As those who die, in short, for something".

Painted in 1972, eight years after the event due to a long and complex development, the work resulted in the black and white style from which the red of the flags rises like a flame among the heartbroken faces of those present, absent living or dead and angels and demons who had idealistically admired that historical figure, with results of deep lyricism: a visionary allegory, rich in powerful symbolic charge for the collective communist imagination, which is also squeezed around the Colosseum for the funeral of Enrico Berlinguer. Guttuso always insisted that this was his most metaphysical painting: it represents death, the being in the twilight of existence. Many red flags waved during the funeral ceremony, lay at the Pantheon, yet religious in the nearby Basilica di Santa Maria Sopra Minerva, revealing the late conversion of feeling which had irresistibly attracted a convinced Marxist who was on the sad threshold of silence. As the red of a poem by Pier Paolo Pasolini which ended, in modern and full verses, thusly:

> But it is inevitable that over these years
> the random becomes final,
> the absolute free will.
> The meanings become crystals:
> and your red, Guttuso, will return to history,
> like a river lost in the desert.
> Your red will be the red, the red of the worker
> and the red of the poet, one red alone
> that will mean the reality of a struggle,
> hope, victory and pity.

Renato Guttuso, *Colosseum*, 1972,
oil on canvas, 102 x 133 cm, Vatican City,
Vatican Museums

Renato Guttuso, *Colosseum (polychrome Colosseum)*, 1972, oil on canvas, 100 x 80 cm, private collection

A Myth of Our Time

Renato Guttuso, *Colosseum*, 1972,
oil on canvas, 130 x 100 cm, Jesi,
Pinacoteca Civica and Galleria di Arte
Contemporanea – Palazzo Pianetti

In this painting, the amphitheatre is taken from
the same perspective as the view that appears
in *The Funeral of Togliatti*.

A Myth of Our Time

Renato Guttuso, *The Funeral of Togliatti*, 1972, collage and acrylic on paper mounted on 4 panels of multilayered wood, 340 x 440 cm, Bologna, MAMbo – Museo d'Arte Moderna di Bologna

A Myth of Our Time

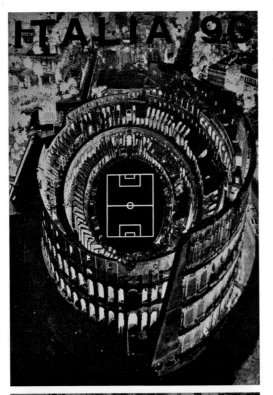

Alberto Burri, *Italy 90*, 1987, series of six official posters realised for the 1990 Football World Cup, paper Fabriano Rosaspina, 100 x 70 cm, offset print

Only the unbridled passion for football, which he nurtured since his early youth in Tiferno, which he knew well and had to support, meant that Alberto Burri, at the apex of his fame, accepted the invitation of Luca Cordero di Montezemolo to create the visual identity of the World Cup in 1990, without demanding any compensation. To represent the temple of cheers he chose what he himself had had described as the oldest and most beautiful stadium the world, a Colosseum reconstruction on the basis of an aerial photo. The image of the amphitheatre was elongated and broken down so it could be placed on the arena floor, like a fine photomontage, a pitch of various colours in the six different versions of the poster, among which one could not miss the beloved black one. The executives of FIFA were enthusiastic about the final result, especially with the specimen in green with the flags of all participating nations – which Burri had procured after careful research – assembled around the field. He paid the project the same care that he had shown in the creation of the works of art, while being aware that is was a communication product, and as effective as a popular illustrated news magazine: meticulous in composition, the study of the shapes cut out from card like in a collage or assemblage, the choice of font (an essential Helvetica "sign") and the colour sequence, the obsessive attention to the processes of print which could obtain a remarkable depth of blacks of the favoured fonts of Corrado Petruzzi in Città di Castello, where a limited and signed edition of the posters was born, and presented to the public and convened journalists in 1987.

The great photographers of the 19th century had challenged artists to paint the Colosseum with light, conferring on its image that innovative smoothness of tonal values, which reached new heights of refined Romanticism, while the many professional campaigns documented a 'posing archaeology'. In the twentieth century and even in the first years of the twenty first it seems that the most immortalised monument in the world, an essential setting for millions of selfies, "a perfect spaceship" which has landed in the heart of Rome, as Marco Delogu happily called it, has awed the gaze of the greatest: for its strength, for the difficulty of understanding it and bringing back the emotion of its bulk and the engulfing enigma of its eternity.

Thus did Josef Koudelka stand on the threshold: it enclosed and protected, like in a reliquary of perspective grids worthy of Bauhaus experiments, a stone which preserves in its contours the elliptical footprint of the monument, and of one of its steps: a synecdoche in the network of lights and shadows cast by the much discussed fences, whose regular geometries are distorted like in an optical pattern of craters in the blocks, caused by the hunger of metal. Olivo Barbieri was able to dominate the engulfing "beast", as the writer Giorgio Manganelli wished to portray it in a thrilling piece, setting it on fire from Heaven, just like one normally only sees in photographs or the air, or from the Oppian Hill on a bright rainy night, stealing "una figura per quinta" from the paintings of Friedrich or Magritte.

Gabriele Basilico manages to find the right shot only at a distance or inside, and Pino Musi, with all the shades of black lowers the horizon towards its underground, for many dark centuries.

For Maurizio Galimberti too, a single point of view of the Colosseum is not enough: with his polaroid he composes a photographic mosaic which he has in mind like a musical score, collecting every aspect of the decomposing monument and gathering them in open volumes between stone and sky.

A Myth of Our Time

Olivo Barbieri, *Rome 1995*

Josef Koudelka, *The Colosseum*, Rome, 2003

A Myth of Our Time

Pino Musi, *Colosseum, Opus*, Rome, 2010

A Myth of Our Time

Maurizio Galimberti, *Cylindrical Colosseum*, Roma 2012, 85 x 58.8 cm, private collection

The long and passionate research of Alfred Seiland is dedicated to reflecting on what survives or lives of the Roman Empire in the world today, and the Colosseum could only be the focus; the Austrian photographer investigates it like in an autopsy, in its current context with the contradictions of modern use, while a cold and deeply personal light pervades the destiny of an icon with alienating examples in various parts of the world.

A self-timer in shorts with a centurion portrays the British Martin Parr in his natural habitat, the human comedy which invades the Piazza del Colosseo, with colourful crowds of tourists who have always come from everywhere, for many years. Close-up without pity frames and therefore consecrates contemporary collective rituals and sharp, consumerist gestures of individuals: microphone guides illustrate how the Colosseum was, showing improbable laminated reconstructions – how elegant indeed was the young lady immortalised in the same pose as Cartier Breton in 1959! – while all are with their heads up with camera raised above the crowd; and also maps, handbags, drinks, hats and fans to shelter from the blazing sun, and the gladiator with a mobile phone incorporated into the cheekpiece; the mobile phosphorescent merchandise takes possession of the sacred soil, religiously placed like votive offerings in the stalls crowded with out of place souvenir junk, as Italy tends to do, in a manner that is a little kitsch.

The age old question of coexistence between the most recent urbanisation and the ruins of antiquity in a "postcard city", that is among the most touristic in the world, Rome has undoubtedly formed the source of inspiration for series of *Alternative Postcards of Rome* by Simon Roberts. The Colosseum, that emblem of classical culture, is a the principal subject of these new objects a good four times, boldly contaminated by handling, overlapping and becoming the vintage backdrop of a fading ordinary way of life.

A Myth of Our Time

Alfred Seiland, *Colosseum, Rome*, Italy, 2010

25th September 1906; Via Frattina 52, Rome – Dear Stannie, (…) Yesterday I went to see the Forum. I sat down on a stone bench overlooking the ruins. It was hot and sunny. Carriages full of tourists, postcard sellers, medal sellers, photograph sellers. I was so moved that I almost fell asleep and had to rise brusquely. I looked at the stone bench ruefully but it was too hard and the grass near the Colosseum was too far. So I went home sadly. Rome reminds me of a man who lives by exhibiting to travellers his grandmother's corpse.

James Joyce, *Letter to Stanislaus Joyce*

Martin Parr, *Statues and tourists at the
Colosseum*, Rome 1993

17th August 1827. [...] The moment other sightseers come to the Colosseum, the traveler's pleasure is almost entirely eclipsed. Instead of being carried away by sublime and absorbing reveries, in spite of himself he observes the foibles of the newcomers, and it seems to him that they have many. Life is reduced to what is in a drawing room: in spite of yourself you listen to the banalities they utter. If I had the power, I would be a tyrant, I would have the Colosseum closed during my sojourns in Rome.

Stendhal, *A Roman Journey*, 1829

A Myth of Our Time

Simon Roberts, *"Words fail me" The Colosseum*, 1989

Simon Roberts, *"Shock!" Flavian Amphitheatre or Colosseum*, 1972

Simon Roberts, *"Still in the land of the living" Rome, The Colosseum taken from S. Francesca Romana*, 1954

A Myth of Our Time

Simon Roberts, *"Trying unusual dishes"*
The Colosseum, 1979

Simon Roberts, *"A walk this afternoon"*
Forum Romanum, 1956

Even Paolo Canevari felt on his shoulders all the weight of classical tradition, a concentration of beauty and history which the Colosseum embodies, shifted in the forms and contemporary consistence of a punctured tyre. The subject is so familiar to the author that in the installation *Popolo di Roma* (it was the formula with which the Emperor addressed his subjects in public discourse) that he had placed a series of worn tyres inscribed with the names of the Caesars on the podium of the Temple of Mars Ultor in the Forum of Augustus, to evoke the scrapping of a system of worn out values. Supporting the load of the rubber Colosseum, like a postmodern Atlantis, is the Roman artist himself, elegantly dressed in the American stereotype of the Italian, the protagonist of a performance planned in 2002 for the streets of Little Italy – the tile *Colossus* refers to the gigantic statue which stood next to the amphitheatre to which it gave its name – and shakes in the room of a Milanese gallery where the marble floor became a place for the iteration of the meaning of overwhelming power.

Overcoming every inhibition, Canevari gets to destroy it within the fiction of a fire, with the inexorable slowness of the flames, realising the terrifying prophecy of the Venerable Bede: *Quamdiu stat Colysaeum stat et Roma, quando cadet et Colysaeum cadet et Roma, quando cadet et Roma cadet et mundus.* The video taken by a fixed videocamera in the setting, like a painting of the Last Judgement, coming from a drawing which seeks to become a physical experience, and thus it is silent because the absence of audio favours the concentration on the event in the image: the cathartic destruction of an icon which has been recognisable for centuries.

A Myth of Our Time

Paolo Canevari, *Colossus*, 2002,
photography by Marco Delogu,
210 x 95 cm, Milan, Galleria
Christian Stein

Paolo Canevari, *Colossus*, 2002,
installation, Milan, Galleria
Christian Stein

After the tyre cut outline-sculptures of the
Colosseum, Paolo Canevari has recently created
design objects in which one can indulge in the games
and levity which is more difficult in art. In designing
original sittings, he still works on the idea of the arch
as the architectural archetype in the history of
civilisation, reiterated in objects of high artistic
craftsmanship which recover the precious shellac
finish of nineteenth century tradition.

A Myth of Our Time

Paolo Canevari, *Burning Colosseum*, 2006,
graphite on paper, 30 x 21 cm

Paolo Canevari, *Burning Colosseum*, 2006,
video stills at 3' 15"

A Myth of Our Time

Pablo Echaurren, *The Big Onion*, 2010,
acrylic on canvas, 118 x 160 cm

A Myth of Our Time

For the streets of the Capital, no less than in an angle in the Rione Monti, Hogre, noted writer of Roman Street Art who does not disdain artist residences in galleries, has replicated this – his representational stencil which combines East and West: an imposing pagoda is grafted in the Colosseum, discovery is the allusion.

Cine-Colosseum

"Oh, I say... Now that we are in Milan, do we finally want to go and see this famous Colosseum? What Colosseum, Colosseum?!". In the salacious jokes of *Totò, Peppino e la malafemmina* (1956) we see the celebrity of a monument whose "brand", for image and visibility, was estimated to be worth over 91 billion euros against the 82 of the Duomo of Milan by recent marketing research. Since becoming one of the world capitals of cinema after the war, for the charm of its millennial history which is embodied in a unique concentration of works of art, for the warmth of its people and folklore, Rome and her emblem, the Colosseum, are an open air set. An inexhaustible number of films give Rome a realistic representation, sometimes an artificial and distorted one in that inaccuracy typical of cinematographic fiction, which both heightens its charm and allows it to exist in the heart and memory.

The Flavian Amphitheatre appears as early as the first documentaries of the Lumière brothers and in the optical experiments of the Roman pioneer Filoteo Albertini at the dawn of the twentieth century, yet it was the *peplum*, or sword-and-sandal genre of American production of the fifties and sixties, to constantly use it at least as a model for gladiatorial games, which epics set in Ancient Rome certainly could not miss: Melvyn LeRoy's *Quo vadis?* (1951), Delmer Daves' *Demetrius and the Gladiators* (1954), Anthony Mann's *The Fall of the Roman Empire* (1964) and standing out from them all for quality is Stanley Kubrick's *Spartacus*, historically possible in an age when the Colosseum was yet to be built. After all, "If there were no Rome, I would dream of her!", exclaimed Laurence Olivier in the film for which, as for the others, the amphitheatre was reconstructed in papier-mâché to criteria decidedly distant from archaeological philology, in the studios of Hollywood or Cinecittà. This was if the stands of the Arena of Verona, used in Richard Fleischer's *Barabbas* (1961), were not available. The most sophisticated digital technologies did however allow Ridley Scott, even with a somewhat questionable script, to film his *Gladiator* (2000) in an unparalleled and immersive setting for which it was also necessary to shoot scenes in a hastily erected amphitheatre in Malta, and inside the Colosseum of Africa, El Jem in Tunisia, which had after all already ended up by mistake on the cover of a noted tourist guide book of Rome.

The Colosseum played an important role in William Wyler's 1953 *Roman Holiday*, which brought Hollywood to the Tiber and contributed to the rebirth of the touristic and romantic image of Rome in America, as well as the spread of the Vespa upon which the two protagonists cheerfully scamper around the monument, the symbol of a city which became a place "of which" and not merely "in which" one told a story. It is the case of *To Rome with Love* by Woody Allen (2012). A synthetic and flashing amphitheatre would be the roundabout in a chaotic nighttime traffic jam of cars under pouring rain and in a roaring race of young motorcyclists, in the finale of Fellini's 1972 *Roma*, evoking the descent of modern hordes of barbarian invaders. Two years earlier Bernardo Bertolucci had completed *The Conformist* – set on the day of Mussolini's death – assimilating the life of the slums which led the moral decay under the Fascist regime between the arches of the Colosseum, while in those same ambulatories the families persecuted by the Germans took refuge in the first masterpieces of Neorealism. Salvo Randone, in Elio Petri's intimist *His Days Are Numbered* (1962), reflects on the meaning of existence under that very *monumentum aere perennius*. In front of the Colosseum, upon the terrace of the Temple of Venus and Rome, the director has Ursula Andress kill her *10th Victim* (1965), a bleached Marcello Mastroianni, an actor of a surreal film which boasts the screenplay of Ennio Flaiano and Tonino Guerra and contains stunning aerial views of the Capital.

A solemn scene from Ridley Scott's
Gladiator (USA, 2000), a film which
helped to revive the fame of the
Colosseum worldwide

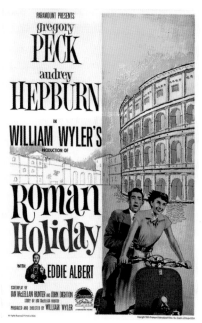

The original poster and a scene from
William Wyler's *Roman Holiday* (USA,
1953), with Gregory Peck and Audrey
Hepburn inside the Colosseum

"Nando stop ... look, have you seen this film? It's the story of a young American who, to get what the world didn't want to give him, yes just like to 'Na', one morning he took it upon himself to climb to the highest point of a skyscraper, sat himself down and said: 'I will jump if they don't give me what I want'. What are you thinking Na', have you thought of something? Do you want to try too, you should find an even higher place Na', find yourself somewhere high Na', and see if they listen, they need to listen!" Thus the Trasteverine simpleton Nando Moriconi, infatuated by the myth of the United States, talking to himself, scales the height of the Colosseum, threatening to jump if they do not allow him to go to America, in the opening sequence of Steno's *An American in Rome* (Italy, 1954). The Colosseum also peers out on the film poster, in which the figure of Alberto Sordi stands out on a chrome motorcycle, with all the irreverent force of his innovative humour which was able to create formidable icons.

The original poster and a scene from
Steno's *Un Americano a Roma* (Italy, 1954)

Kung fu could hardly fail to insert itself into the tradition of the *munera* which took place within the arena: behold the 1972 *Way of the Dragon*, the epic – for fans of the genre – final clash between Chuck Norris and Bruce Lee, who tracks down and faces his rival between the majestic brick vaults. A long, sunlit sequences of images reveal every angle of the Colosseum in Nathan Juran's 1957 *20 Million Miles to Earth*, in which a gigantic plastic reptile tries to climb the monument – like the good King King had done on the Empire State Building – until he is killed by a salvo of bazookas and machine guns: the outcome is expected and fatal for the destruction of the summit of the building, already damaged by the monster who, like a new Polyphemus, seeks in his defence to hurl blocks from it upon American soldiers gathered around in the desolate Piazza.

If these films confirm the choice of the Colosseum as an absolutely key allegory, they are dated primarily due to the lack of technical means at the time, for which the various sequences betray a daring visual synthesis between the scenes shot and the architectural features in the background, the genre of *disaster film* reaches its peak in the catastrophic and charming *The Core*, directed by Jon Amile in 2003, in which the prophecy of the Venerable Bede seems to at last be fulfilled, among eye-popping special effects created lightning and thunderbolts, with the disintegration of the amphitheatre. It was to the great monument that the young heroes of Doug Liman's *Jumper* were launched by teleportation, in a Science Fiction film adapted from a novel by Steven Gould.

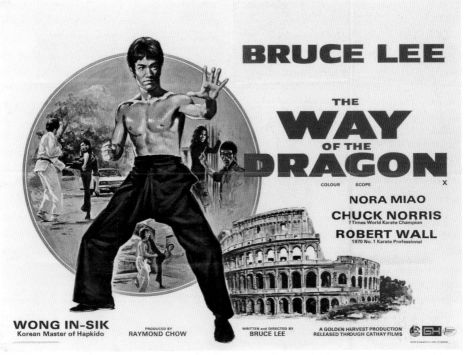

A no holds barred fight from *The Way of the Dragon*, directed by Bruce Lee, USA, 1972

The giant lizard Ymir, after daring
adventures in the city, attempts to seek his
escape atop the Colosseum in Nathan
Juran's *20 Million Miles to Earth*, USA, 1957

Deadly electrical discharges will soon
reduce the Colosseum to dust in Jon
Amiel's *The Core*, USA, 2003

Cine-Colosseum

The poster of *They Call Me Jeeg*, an award-winning film by Gabriele Mainetti, released in Italy in 2016

Less apocalyptic yet more desperate is the the threat of destruction brought to the harsh urban reality of Gerry, the character around which Nico D'Alessandro's 1987 cult film *L'imperatore di Roma* revolves: he appears to imitate the gesture of the Duce to the Velian by raising, at dusk, the pickaxe on the Caelian with the Colosseum behind, but it is only a gesture of an outcast who lives under the stars and finds refuge in the monument. No less dramatic and raw is the Rome revealed with narrative tension by Gabriele Mainetti in the recent *They Call Me Jeeg*: in the last, lunar scene Enzo, by now presumed dead, recognised as a hero, watches over Rome from the summit of the Colosseum and, resolved to defend her under his sweater mask, leaps into the city. A decadent vision of society, not less tragic than upper class Rome, pervades the aesthetic sequences of Paolo Sorrentino's *La Grande Bellezza*, on which Jep Gambardella continues to meditate before the wondrous sight of the Colosseum.

Toni Servillo is Jep Gambardella
in Paolo Sorrentino's *La Grande Bellezza*,
Italy, 2003

Bibliography

On the Colosseum and its fortune

F. Colagrossi, *L'Anfiteatro Flavio nei suoi venti secoli di storia*, Florence-Rome 1913.

M. Di Macco, *Il Colosseo. Funzione simbolica, storica, urbana*, Rome 1971.

P. Quennell, *Il Colosseo*, I Templi della Grandezza, Milan 1973 (ed. or. 1971).

P.G. Guzzo (ed.), *Il Colosseo*, "Archeo" dossier, 21, November 1986.

M.L. Conforto *et al.*, *Anfiteatro Flavio. Immagine, Testimonianze, Spettacoli*, Rome 1988.

Roma. Il Colosseo, Grand Tour di Franco Maria Ricci, 1989.

C. Moatti, *Roma antica. Tra mito e scoperta*, Milan 1992 (ed. or. Paris 1989).

R. Luciani, *Il Colosseo. Architettura, storia, spettacoli e curiosità dell'Anfiteatro Flavio, il più celebre tra i monumenti dell'antichità romana*, Novara 1990.

A. Gabucci (a cura di), *Il Colosseo*, Milan 1999.

I. Insolera, A.M. Sette, *Frondose arcate, Il Colosseo prima dell'archeologia*, exhibition catalogue (Rome, Museo Nazionale Romano, Palazzo Altemps, 18th December 2000 - 18th February 2001), Milan 2000.

R. Rea (ed.), *Rota Colisei. La valle del Colosseo attraverso i secoli*, Milan 2002.

G. Caneva (ed.), *Amphitheatrum Naturae. Il Colosseo, storia e ambienti letti attraverso la sua flora*, Milan 2004.

C. de Seta, *Il Colosseo. Un simbolo della coscienza europea*, Rome 2004.

K. Hopkins, M. Beard, *Il Colosseo. La storia e il mito*, Rome-Bari, 2006 (ed. or. 2005).

F. Coarelli (ed.), *Divus Vespasianus. Il bimillenario dei Flavi*, exhibition catalogue (Rome, Colosseum, Curia and the "Neronian" Cryptoporticus, 27th March 2009 - 10th January 2010), Milan 2009.

M. Borelli (ed.), *Colosseo. Due tre cose che so di lui*, Rome 2015.

M. Poma, *Alla scoperta del Colosseo. Tra mito e realtà*, Arezzo 2015.

L. Frazzoni (ed.), *Colosseo. Biografia di un capolavoro*, "Archeo" monography, June 2016.

M. Polidoro, *L'avventura del Colosseo*, Milan 2016.

On the Shows and the Gladiators

D. Augenti, *Spettacoli del Colosseo nelle cronache degli antichi*, Rome 2001.

A. La Regina (ed.), *Sangue e arena*, exhibition catalogue (Rome, Colosseum, 22nd June 2001 - 7th January 2002), Milan 2001.

F. Meijer, *Un giorno al Colosseo. Il mondo dei gladiatori*, Rome-Bari 2004 (ed. or. Amsterdam 2003).

F. Guidi, *Morte nell'arena. Storia e leggenda dei gladiatori*, Milan 2006.

Ch. Mann, *I gladiatori*, Bologna 2014 (ed. or. München 2013).

On the Artists of the Colosseum

G. Ciucci, *Gli architetti e il fascismo*, Turin 1989.

A. Wilton, I. Bignamini, *Grand Tour. Il fascino dell'Italia nel XVIII secolo*, exhibition catalogue (Rome, Palazzo delle Esposizioni, 5th February - 7th April 1997), Milan 1997.

R. Bossaglia (ed.), *Ritratto di un'idea. Arte e architettura nel Fascismo*, exhibition catalogue (Rome, Palazzo Valentini, 11th May - 22nd September 2002), Milan 2002.

Maestà di Roma da Napoleone all'Unità d'Italia, Da Ingres a Degas. Gli artisti francesi a Roma (exhibition catalogue, Rome, Villa Medici, 7th March - 29th June 2003), Milan 2003.

M. Makarius, *Ruins*, Paris 2004.

C. de Seta (ed.), *Imago Urbis Romae. L'immagine di Roma in età moderna*, exhibition catalogue (Rome, Musei Capitolini, 11th February - 15th May 2005), Milan 2005.

F.P. Fiore, A. Nesselrath (ed.), *La Roma di Leon Battista Alberti. Umanisti, architetti e artisti alla scoperta dell'antico nella città del Quattrocento*, exhibition catalogue (Roma, Musei Capitolini, 24th June - 16th October 2005), Milan 2005.

A. Lo Bianco, A. Negro, *Il Settecento a Roma*, exhibition catalogue (Rome, Palazzo Venezia, 10th November 2005 - 26th February 2006), Cinisello Balsamo 2005.

G. Martini (ed.), *I luoghi del cinema*, Milan 2005.

C. de Seta, *Roma, cinque secoli di vedute*, Naples 2006.

E. Gentile, *Fascismo di pietra*, Rome-Bari 2007.

P. Nicoloso, *Mussolini architetto*, Turin 2008.

P. D'Agostini, *Commedia*, Dictionary of Cinema, Milan 2009.

C. Brook, V. Curzi, *Roma e l'Antico. Realtà e visione nel '700*, exhibition catalogue (Rome, Fondazione Roma Museo, Palazzo Sciarra, 30th November 2010 - 6th March 2011), Milan 2010.

A. Marchi, M.R. Valazzi, *La città ideale. L'utopia del Rinascimento a Urbino tra Piero della Francesca e Raffaello*, exhibition catalogue (Urbino, Galleria Nazionale delle Marche, 6th April - 8th July 2012), Milan 2012.

J. Stewart, *Street Art Stories. Roma*, Rome 2012.

V. Greene (ed.), *Italian Futurism 1909-1944. Reconstructing the Universe*, exhibition catalogue (New York, Guggenheim Museum, 21st February - 1st September 2014), New York 2014.

P. Manfren, *Archeologia e simboli della "romanitas" nella pubblicistica e nella grafica fascista: il caso de "La Rivista Illustrata del Popolo d'Italia" (1923-1943)*, in "Tecla", 10, 2014, pp. 24-61.

M. Barbanera, A. Capodiferro, *La forza delle rovine*, exhibition catalogue (Rome, Museo Nazionale Romano, Palazzo Altemps, 8th October 2015 - 31st January 2016), Milan 2015.

A. Campitelli, M. Frassineti, *Street Art a Roma. Come cambia la città*, Rome 2015.

V. Crippa (texts), F. Ferri, L. Romano (photography), *Roberto Bolle. Viaggio nella bellezza*, Milan 2015.

V. Viadotto, *Esposizione Universale Roma. Una città nuova dal Fascismo agli anni '60*, exhibition catalogue (Rome, Museo dell'Ara Pacis, 12th March - 14th June 2015), Rome 2015.

C. Crescentini, C. D'Orazio, F. Pirani (ed.), *Roma Pop City 60-67*, exhibition catalogue (Rome, MACRO, Museo d'Arte Contemporanea Roma, 13th July - 27th November 2016), Rome 2016.

M. Delogu (ed.), *Roma, il mondo. Fotografia. Festival internazionale di Roma, Quindicesima edizione* (Rome, MACRO, Museo d'Arte Contemporanea Roma, 21st October 2016 - 8th January 2017), Macerata 2016.

S. Chiodi, *Il palazzo come immagine*, in M. Piazza (ed.), *Il Palazzo della Civiltà Italiana*, Milan 2017.

A. Galansino (ed.), *Ai Weiwei. Libero*, exhibition catalogue (Florence, Palazzo Strozzi, 23rd September 2016 - 22nd January 2017), Florence 2016.

R. Ash, *Sir Lawrence Alma-Tadema*, New York 1989.

E. Becker, E. Prettejohn, *Sir Lawrence Alma-Tadema*, exhibition catalogue (Amsterdam-Liverpool), Amsterdam 1996.

R.J. Barrow, *Lawrence Alma-Tadema*, London 2001.

E. Querci, S. De Caro, *Alma Tadema e la nostalgia dell'antico*, exhibition catalogue (Naples, Museo Archeologico Nazionale, 19th October 2007 - 31st March 2008), Milan 2007.

F. Fabiani (ed.), *Olivo Barbieri. Immagini 1978-2014*, exhibition catalogue (Rome, MAXXI, Museo Nazionale delle Arti del XXI secolo, 29th May - 15th November 2015), Venice 2015.

M. Delogu (ed.), *Olivo Barbieri, site specific_ROMA 04 14*, Rome 2015.

C. Sarteanesi (ed.), *Burri. Catalogo generale. Opera grafica 1949-1994*, Fondazione Palazzo Albizzini, Collezione Burri, Città di Castello 2016.

A. Scarpa, *Caffi. Luci del Mediterraneo*, exhibition catalogue (Belluno-Rome, 2005-2006), Milan 2005.

AA.VV., *Paolo Canevari*, Milan 2002.

D. Eccher (ed.), *Paolo Canevari. Nothing from Nothing*, catalogo della mostra (Rome, MACRO, Museo d'Arte Contemporanea Roma, 25th May - 30th September 2007), Milan 2007.

G. Celant (ed.), *Paolo Canevari*, exhibition catalogue (Prato, Centro per l'Arte Contemporanea "Luigi Pecci", 20th March - 1st August 2010), Milan 2010.

K. Monrad (ed.), *Christoffer Wilhelm Eckersberg*, exhibition catalogue (Copenhagen, Statens Museum for Kunst, 8th October 2015 - 24th February 2016), München-London-New York 2015.

M. Bussagli, F, Giudiceandrea (ed.), *Escher*, exhibition catalogue (Bologna, Palazzo Albergati, 12th March - 19th July 2015), Milan 2015.

M. Bussagli, F, Giudiceandrea (ed.), *Escher*, exhibition catalogue (Milan, Palazzo Reale, 24th June 2016 - 22nd January 2017), Milan 2016.

B. Donato (ed.), *Maurizio Galimberti. Paesaggio Italia*, exhibition catalogue (Venice, Istituto Veneto di Scienze, Lettere ed Arti, Palazzo Franchetti, 16th February - 12th May 2013), Venice 2013.

L. des Cars, D. de Font-Réaulx, É. Papet, *The Spectacular Art of Jean-Léon Gérome (1824-1904)*, exhibition catalogue (Los Angeles, Paris, Madrid 2010-2011), Paris 2010.

F. Carapezza Guttuso (ed.), *Guttuso. Capolavori dai Musei*, exhibition catalogue (Turin, Palazzo Bricherasio, 18th February - 29th May 2005), Milan 2005.

G. Faroult, C. Voiriot (ed.), *Hubert Robert. 1733-1808. Un peintre visionnaire*, exhibition catalogue (Paris, Musée du Louvre, 8th March - 30th May 2016), Paris 2016.

M. Morgan Grasselli, Y. Jackall (ed.), *Hubert Robert*, exhibition catalogue (Washington, National Gallery of Art, 26th June - 2nd October 2016), London 2016.

M. Trier (texts by), *Alfred Seiland. Imperium Romanum. Opus Extractum*, Ostfildern 2013.

Superstudio. La vita segreta del Monumento Continuo. Conversazioni con Gabriele Mastrigli, Macerata 2015.

Literary sources

G.G. Belli, *Sonetti*, edited by G. Vivolo, with the collaboration of P. Gibellini, Mondadori, Milan 1978.

G.G. Byron, *Manfredi*, translation by G. Manganelli, Einaudi, Turin 2000.

F.-R. de Chateaubriand, *Viaggio in Italia*, translation by P. Tucci, Carocci, Rome 2010.

Ch. Dickens, *Impressioni italiane*, translation by C.M. Messina, Robin Edizioni, Rome-Turin 2005.

E. Gibbon, *Storia della decadenza e caduta dell'impero romano*, translation by G. Frizzi, Einaudi, Turin 1967.

J.W. Goethe, *Viaggio in Italia*, translation by G.V. Amoretti, UTET, Turin 1965.

J.W. Goethe, *Viaggio in Italia (1786-1788)*, translation by E. Zaniboni, Rizzoli, Milan 1991.

F. Gregorovius, *Diari romani*, edited by A.M. Arpino, Avanzini and Torraca, Rome 1967.

N. Hawthorne, *Il fauno di marmo*, translation by G. Spina, Rizzoli, Milan 1961.

H. James, *Daisy Miller*, translation by D. Meneghelli, Einaudi, Turin 1999.

Madame de Staël, *Corinna o l'Italia*, translation by A.E. Signorini, Mondadori, Milan 2006.

E.A. Poe, *Tutti i racconti e le poesie*, translation by C. Izzo, Casini, Rome 1953.

G. Rodari, *L'uomo che rubava il Colosseo*, Edizioni EL, San Dorligo della Valle 2013.

M. Sorgi, *Colosseo Vendesi. Una storia incredibile ma non troppo*, Bompiani, Milan 2016.

Stendhal, *Passeggiate romane*, translation by M. Colesanti, Garzanti, Milan 2004.

M. Twain, *Gli innocenti all'estero*, translation by S. Neri, Feltrinelli, Milan 2001.

É. Zola, *Diario di viaggio*, translation by i C. Montrésor, Electa/Gallimard, Milan 1992.

É. Zola, *Roma*, edizioni Sten, Turin 1923.

Le traduzioni delle altre pagine d'autore presenti nell'antologia sono tratte da *Il Colosseo e la letteratura* in P. Quennell, *Il Colosseo*, Mondadori, Milan 1973 (ed. or. 1971).

The English edition quotes are taken from the following sources

Byron, *Manfred* [John Murray] (London 1817).

Deakin, Richard, *Flora of the Colosseum in Rome*, London, 1855.

De Chateaubriand, Francois-Rene, *Voyage en Italie*, trans. Kline, A.S [Poetry in Translation] (2010).

De Staël, *Corinne*, trans. Hill, I [Bell and Bradfute] (Edinburgh 1833).

Dickens, Charles, *Pictures from Italy*, London, 1846.

Gibbon, *The Decline and Fall of the Roman Empire*, London, 1782.

Goethe, *Italian Journey*, trans. W. Halsey, F in *Seeing Europe with Famous Authors*, W. Halsey, F (ed.) [Funk & Wagnalls Company] (New York and London 1914).

Gregorovius, *The Roman Journals of Ferdinand Gregorovius*, trans. Hamilton, G. W. [G. Bell & Sons] (London 1911)

James, Henry, *Daisy Miller, A Study* [Harper & Brothers] (New York 1878)

Joyce, James, *Letter to Brother Stanislaus,* 25th September 1906.

Hawthorne, Nathaniel, *The Marble Faun* [Ticknor and Fields] (Boston 1860).

Longfellow, Henry Wadsworth, *Michael Angelo: A Dramatic Poem,* Boston, 1884

Martial, *The Epigrams,* trans. C. A. Ker, Walter [Loeb Classical Library] (London 1919).

Poe, Edgar Allan, *The Colosseum,* in *The Baltimore Saturday Visitor,* Baltimore, 1833.

Stendhal, *A Roman Journal,* trans. Chevalier, H [Pickle Partners Publishing] (1957)

Tertullian, *De Spectaculis,* trans. Glover, T. R [Loeb Classical Library] (London 1977)

Twain, Mark, *The Innocents Abroad, or, The Pilgrim's Progress* [H. H. Bancroft and Company] (San Francisco 1869).

Verri, Alessandro, *Roman Nights, or the Tomb of the Scipios,* trans. Hilliard, Henry W. [John Ball] (Philadelphia 1850).

Zola, Émile, *Rome,* trans. Vizetelly, E. A. (London 1896)